THE FORMATION
OF CHRISTIAN
UNDERSTANDING

THE FORMATION OF CHRISTIAN UNDERSTANDING

Theological Hermeneutics

by

CHARLES M. WOOD

Wipf & Stock
PUBLISHERS
Eugene, Oregon

Wipf and Stock Publishers
199 West 8th Avenue, Suite 3
Eugene, Oregon 97401

The Formation of Christian Understanding
Theological Hermeneutics
By Wood, Charles M.
Copyright©1993 by Wood, Charles M.
ISBN: 1-57910-336-7
Publication date 3/9/2000
Previously published by Trinity Press Intl, 1993

Contents

Preface to the Second Edition

Common wisdom has it that readers do not read prefaces. I overlooked this wisdom in the original edition of this book and said some things in the preface that I meant to be read. In a couple of pages, I explained the overall purpose and approach of the book before going on to acknowledge various debts. At the risk of absurdity, let me implore the reader of this edition to read both this preface and the original preface before plunging ahead to the first chapter.

This is a second edition, not a revised edition, of a book first published in 1981. If I were starting the book over, a good deal of work produced over the last dozen years on the themes with which it deals would have to be taken into account. My own reading of this more recent work, however, has generally served to reconfirm rather than to call into question the basic approach I have taken here, and to convince me that there is as great a need now as there was then for a clear statement of this approach.

If I were to undertake a revision, I might be tempted to qualify some fairly forthright statements in this book and say some other things a little differently for the sake of easier comparison and contrast with other current developments in theological hermeneutics and to show that I have been paying attention. (For a survey of some of those developments, see my article, "Theological Hermeneutics," *Quarterly Review* 7/3 [Fall 1987]: 91-100.) I am glad not to be faced with that temptation. There is value in leaving the text relatively uncluttered so that the main lines of the argument are left as clear as possible.

In any case, the main thing I would want to say to the new reader, in light of the reception accorded the original edition, can just as easily be said here: The book should be read as a whole, and each chapter in the light of the other chapters. For example, what is said in chapter II about the existential, self-transforming character of the knowledge of God should be kept in mind when, in chapter IV, we come to a consideration of the way biblical texts may function to disclose the reality of God. Similarly, what is said about the canonical sense and use of scripture in chapter III and about the elaboration of a canonical construal in chapter IV should be recalled when chapter V takes up the matter of how biblical texts themselves are rightly subject to criticism in the light of the knowledge of God which the Bible yields.

Some reviewers of the original edition remarked that while the vocabulary of the book is often conservative, and some attention is given to what we might be able to learn from the church's older exegetical principles and practices as well as from our contemporaries, the implications of the proposal set forth are quite radical and liberating. While I am not sure that either "conservative" or "radical" is an especially useful term, I agree with the tenor of those remarks. Those reviewers, and readers like them, were able to make the appropriate connections among the book's principal points. The book represents a venture in postcritical hermeneutics. This means no abandonment of the critical spirit—if anything, a reaffirmation of it with a new scope and depth, in the pursuit of a genuinely theological reading of scripture. It is my hope that readers from a great variety of theological perspectives will find something useful here.

There is one point that I would certainly put differently if I were writing the book now and, although it is not of major importance so far as the argument of the book is concerned, it is worth mentioning. In two places—pages 28 and 82—I define Christian theology as "a critical inquiry into the truthfulness of Christian witness," and I say that this inquiry involves two basic sorts of questions: questions as to whether that witness is truly Christian, and questions as to whether it is true. I have since come to believe that the inquiry involves three rather than two sorts of questions, the third being questions as to the fitting enactment of Christian witness, or as to whether what is said and done as Christian witness is fitting to the context. I also now believe "validity" to be a more adequate term than "truthfulness" as a general designation for what it is that Christian theology aims to determine about Christian witness. These revisions represent an evolution or further articulation of the earlier position rather than a more fundamental change. (I have developed a fuller account of this understanding of Christian theology in *Vision and Discernment: An Orientation in Theological Study* [Atlanta: Scholars Press, 1985].)

I am very grateful to those readers whose encouragement provided the impetus for this reissue of the book, and to Dr. Harold W. Rast and his colleagues at Trinity Press International for undertaking it.

C.M.W.

Preface to the First Edition

My purpose in these chapters is to set forth in brief a coherent perspective on the Christian interpretation and use of the Bible. This is, then, an essay in theological hermeneutics. That often troublesome and intimidating word, "hermeneutics," is here to be taken in its old conventional sense, as designating, simply, the discipline of interpretation: hermeneutics is critical reflection upon the practice of interpretation—its aims, conditions, and criteria. The adjective "theological" before the noun indicates that in this case such critical reflection is to be informed by theological considerations. That is, rather than asking in general how the biblical text may be understood or what values may be realized in its interpretation, theological hermeneutics asks more specifically how the text may be Christianly understood and what the aims of a deliberate Christian use of it might be. Of course, these specifically theological questions are to be pursued within the context of general hermeneutical reflection upon the problems and possibilities of textual interpretation, but the exact relationship of the theological inquiry to that context is always at issue and cannot be taken for granted.

To speak in this way of "theological hermeneutics" (rather than, say, "biblical hermeneutics") is to acknowledge pluralism in interpretation. We have come to realize that practically any body of literature, including the Bible, may be explored and exploited in a variety of ways. No single interpretative strategy is likely to be granted exclusive rights to a literary region. It is therefore urgent that we learn to ask ourselves, with increasing directness and incisiveness, what we are about in interpretation. Granted that any number of understandings of the biblical text are possible, legitimate, and valuable in their own ways, how are we to describe, seek, and appropriate that understanding (or that collection of understandings) of it which is proper to our use of it as Christian scripture? It is to this basic question that this book is addressed. To attend to this question in any depth is to encounter such standard problems as that of the relationship between the modern critical study of the Bible and its use as the Christian canon; but it is also to have a standpoint from which to deal creatively with such problems so that they may be perceived as opportunities for a critically enhanced reconception of Christian affirmations concerning the status and functions of scripture.

Chapter I was previously published in the *Perkins Journal*, Spring 1980. I thank its editor, Prof. Leroy T. Howe, for permission to reprint it as well as for his reading of the entire manuscript. Drafts of Chapters II and IV were presented to gatherings at Yale in March 1980. I am grateful for the critical discussions on those occasions, and I am particularly grateful to Prof. Hans W. Frei for his generous hospitality and unfailing helpfulness. To colleagues at Perkins School of Theology—particularly Profs. Victor Paul Furnish, Virgil P. Howard, and Schubert M. Ogden —I am indebted for their comments on portions of the book. Naturally I absolve all of these from responsibility for its shortcomings. Thanks are also due Ms. Sally A. Snow for her cheerful and capable typing of the manuscript.

C.M.W.

I
The Task
of
Theological Hermeneutics

In his 1905 Nathaniel William Taylor Lectures at Yale, William Newton Clarke observed: "There is a strange magic about the work of interpreting a book with which one feels bound always to agree. The process is not favorable to the ascertainment of truth."[1] A growing awareness of this magic and a growing determination to resist its power were among the factors which, within the previous two centuries, had led to a deliberate separation between the scholarly interpretation of religious texts and their religious use. The enchantment was broken by a twofold strategy: One step is to regard the text in question as a writing with which one might after all responsibly disagree, that is, as a human work rather than, say, as the literal Word of God. If the text is at least in some respects a human production, then one may engage with it critically at least in those respects. The second, and perhaps more decisive, step is to identify the aims and methods of one's study of the text in such a way that the question of one's agreement or disagreement with the text simply does not arise as a factor in that inquiry. The development of modern biblical scholarship as preeminently a descriptive historical study incorporates this strategic step.

As Sevareid's Law so aptly puts it, the chief cause of problems is solutions. The separation between the interpretation of texts and their religious appropriation encouraged the proliferation and refinement of interpretative techniques, resulting in vastly increased knowledge of the texts, their authorship, background, editorial history, literary form and content. It was also to pose a hermeneutical question with what appeared to be new depth and urgency: Just what does it mean to understand a text? What is the goal of interpretation? Formerly, when understanding flowed more or less directly into appropriation, an interpreter had some sense of what an adequate interpretation involved; there was a use to be served. But once the task of the scholarly interpretation of religious texts has been severed in principle from the religious use of those texts, the question of what constitutes a valid understanding of a text comes into new prominence. The modern study of "general hermeneutics" arose in response to that question; and though the form of the inquiry was often markedly Kantian ("How is understanding possible?"), the question that impelled the inquiry was the one set by this new situation: What is it to understand a text, apart from any specific employment of it?

That question is problematic in the extreme. To understand something is, after all, to have some specific abilities with regard to it. To understand a map is ordinarily to be able to find one's way around by it. To understand an order is to be able to obey it if conditions permit, or to know what obeying it would involve. To understand algebra is to be able to perform and apply various mathematical operations in appropriate circumstances, and to know when and why a particular operation is right or wrong. In each of these cases, a "fuller" understanding than that sketched so incompletely here would still be capable of description in terms of specific abilities and capacities. And it is normal to depict the understanding of written works in similar terms, and to use the presence or absence of certain abilities as marks by which to judge whether or not a person has understood the writing. One who understands a text will be able to make use of the text in ways that demonstrate—and in some sense even constitute—understanding. (That is, one's understanding of the text is not something that lurks behind one's abilities to deal with it in various ways. One's understanding *is* one's abilities, and the measure of one's abilities is the exercise of them.)

Given these features of the concept of understanding, it is not difficult to see why the severance of the task of interpretation from the ordinary context of a writing's use creates some perplexity. Nor is the ensuing merger of hermeneutics with epistemology surprising. The desire to deal with understanding apart from application reinforced the tendency which the grammar of our language already seems to give us to regard understanding as the name of a phenomenon, a mental state or process which might be experienced, as it were, in the privacy of one's own mind, apart from any practical entanglements or consequences. A notion of understanding as basically a recognition, a replication in the interpreter's mind of that which is understood, came into prominence in the ongoing discussion of general hermeneutics. The subsequent course of this discussion, and the fortunes of this notion of understanding within it, cannot be traced in any detail here. But it is noteworthy that in its more recent phases it has been significantly affected by adopting such claims as that there is no understanding without existential engagement, and that understanding itself already involves appropriation. That is, one of the most intriguing developments in recent general hermeneutics is the acknowledgment that the question of one's understanding of a text cannot be intelligibly discussed apart from the question of the use one has made or is prepared to make of it.

A word of caution here: Important as it is to relate understanding and use, it is crucial not to identify them in such a way as to imply that to understand a text is to agree with it, so that, for example, only a Buddhist could understand the Platform Sutra, only a Presbyterian could understand the Westminster Confession, or only a person who obeys an order has truly understood it. It is crucial to remember that understanding has to do with abilities, and that abilities may be demonstrated in various ways. One who refuses to obey an order may *thereby* demonstrate an understanding of it—perhaps an understanding superior to that of someone who obeys blindly. A Buddhist who declines to affirm the Apostles' Creed may nevertheless show an understanding of it in a variety of appropriate ways. In such cases it is still what one is able to do with the object in question that allows a judgment as to the adequacy of one's understanding of it. A text can also be misunderstood, certainly; but the recognition of misunderstanding presupposes criteria of right understanding which may be violated. The point is that these criteria may be satisfied by quite divergent uses of a given text, including uses by those who withhold agreement. These alternative uses, too, constitute engagement and appropriation, however unconventional.

Of course, theorists in the modern hermeneutical tradition since its late-eighteenth-century beginning have generally affirmed that understanding does lead to something, that it has a use. Often this outcome has been described in terms of the enhancement of the quality of one's life and thus of one's culture; the ongoing humanization of the race is effected through the sort of growth which the task of understanding, as well as its accomplishment, provide. At the same time, the working interpreters of various bodies of literature, both religious and secular, who have often remained at some distance from the highly theoretical reflections of hermeneuticians, have felt little reluctance to specify the goals of their own interpretative efforts in terms of the uses they hope to make of their texts. Even those early advocates of free critical study of the Bible who established that twofold strategy of separation previously discussed still carried on their own investigations in such a way as to produce what they considered usable results. They only needed some freedom from a constricting tradition of interpretation, some room to maneuver, so that they could make the text available for use in some different ways, ways that seemed to them more promising.

What all this suggests is that "understanding a text" may be no single thing after all. What constitutes understanding depends a great deal on the use one wants to make of the text, as well as on the character of the text itself. The varied understandings of which a given text is patient cannot always be ordered on a scale from greater to less; they may simply be different. The cab driver and the cartographer may have somewhat different understandings of the same map. Each is a specialist. The historian and the believer may cultivate differing abilities with regard to the same scriptural material because each has a different use to make of it, and these two understandings might not compete or conflict. (Then again, they might, in a particular instance. There are likely to be complex relationships and interdependences among such uses.) To speak of a variety of understandings of a single text is not to claim that *any* understanding of a text is a valid one. It is rather to presume that, since a text may have various valid uses, it may be less misleading to speak of various understandings appropriate to these several uses than to identify one use as that in connection with which the term "understanding" may be employed. It is, of course, tempting to reserve the term for

that particular use of the text with which one is especially
concerned, as a way of putting other uses in their place. But
that maneuver is increasingly discreditable.

An explicit acknowledgment of the relationship between
understanding and use can have some important consequences for the discipline of interpretation known as theological hermeneutics. Among these consequences is a more
adequate way of distinguishing this discipline from other
hermeneutical inquiries. The various subfields of hermeneutics (often called "local" or "special" hermeneutics)
have commonly been distinguished with respect to their
subject matter, that is, the sort of text with which each one
deals. Each local hermeneutics accommodates the principles of general hermeneutics to the peculiar features of a
given sort of material. Legal hermeneutics has to do with
the interpretation of legal texts, literary hermeneutics with
literary works, religious hermeneutics with religious texts.
One problem with this division of fields is that it fails to deal
adequately with the fact that a single text or type of text
may be put to different uses. Religious texts, for example,
may be studied "as literature," as historical documents, as
psychological records, and so forth, as well as with regard
to their religious character (however that is conceived).
Even considered as religious texts, they may be interpreted
quite differently by those who use them as such in a religious community, on the one hand, and by students of the
history of religions, on the other. The situation is further
complicated by the fact that all sorts of texts may become
religious texts by adoption.

Hence there may be significant differences between the
concerns of Christian theological hermeneutics and the
concerns of other hermeneutical inquiries which have the
same texts in view. Those differences will be more readily
recognized and honored if the specific aims of theological

hermeneutics, as distinct from these other efforts, are articulated. The logical hermeneutics is not simply the application of a general theory of interpretation to a specific kind of text. Nor is it a special theory of interpretation tailored to a unique kind of text. (Advocates of a "sacred hermeneutics" have typically argued that these texts are of so special a character that they require an entirely distinct discipline of interpretation. This approach may finally come to be regarded as a misplaced effort.) Theological hermeneutics is, instead, a reflection upon the aims and conditions of what may be called the "Christian understanding" of Christian scripture and tradition, recognizing that there may also be other understandings of this material serving other uses. The term "Christian understanding" is meant to call attention to the fact that Christians, as Christians, have certain ways of relating to and dealing with these texts, just as a different constellation of interests and purposes may lead one to pursue a "historical understanding" or a "literary understanding" of the same texts. "Christian understanding" is not a privileged, esoteric knowledge; it is, like these others, simply an understanding whose criteria are informed by the particular aims and interests that motivate it.

Theological hermeneutics begins by asking what sorts of abilities constitute the possibility of the distinctively Christian use or uses of these texts, and goes on to ask how these abilities are gained and strengthened. The first task of theological hermeneutics, then, is not to delimit and describe the material to be interpreted—material that may be shared with any number of studies—but rather to inquire into the character of Christian understanding. This does not mean that the nature of the material is irrelevant, for certainly the character of Christian understanding is intimately bound up with the character of the texts upon which it is nourished and exercised. The point is simply that the actuality of Christian interaction with these texts, and the understanding that results from this interaction and guides further interaction, cannot be deduced from the obvious features of the texts themselves. Both too much and too little may be obvious.

This discussion has proceeded thus far without any invocation of the term "meaning." In view of the prominence of that term in much hermeneutical discussion, the omission itself deserves some mention. It is commonly asserted that the goal of interpretation is to understand the meaning of the text, as if "meaning" were the object of "understanding." This formula has seemingly promised relief from the pressing question as to how to define the aim of interpretation without reference to a text's employment. Implicit in the formula is the notion that meaning is a property of a text: the text means. But this is surely misleading. In correct usage, the phrase, "The text means . . ." is always elliptical. What the phrase obscures is the connection between the text and its user or users: those who mean something *by* it (for instance, its author) and those *to* whom it means something (its readers and interpreters). There is no escape from the issue of the text's uses, despite the illusory security of "the meaning of the text." Of course, in dealing with many classes of utterances, the context in which they are spoken, heard, read, or studied specifies whose use and what sort of use is to be regarded. But even very simple utterances can have multiple "meanings"; and with a text of any complexity at all, especially if it has had a long history of varied readings and uses, the elliptical phrase is best avoided altogether. "Understanding the meaning of a text," for all its promise, is cumbersome and deceptive. It is crucial to identify the particular use or uses of the text with which one is concerned, and then—recognizing that "understanding" always refers to the acquisition or possession of determinate, or at least determinable, abilities with regard to its object —to specify the sort of understanding at issue. The term "meaning" can then drop out of prominence and assume a less conspicuous and more modest function in the discussion of interpretation.

Accordingly, it is the Christian uses of Christian texts with which we are concerned here. It should go without saying that Christians, as Christians, have many uses for these texts, and that some of these overlap with the uses other interpreters make of them. The Christian understanding of the texts, broadly conceived, includes elements of historical, philosophical, literary, and other sorts of understanding. It is subject to enrichment as well as correction by developments in the disciplines concerned with each of these modes of interpretation. The boundaries between "Christian understanding" and these other inquiries are neither fixed nor impermeable. Insofar as the Christian use of a text involves historical knowledge, for example, those concerned with the Christian use have more than a passing interest in the fortunes of historical scholarship. The phrase "Christian understanding" is not meant to isolate a particular approach from all others, but to indicate a distinctive family of "understandings." Theological hermeneutics has some peculiar responsibility to illuminate those components of Christian understanding which are largely disregarded in other major approaches to the texts, and to place those components in their relationship with other members of the family.

It would be a mistake, then, to assume that there is a discrete, unitary phenomenon called "Christian understanding," whose nature and whose relationship to certain texts we are now to investigate. "Christian understanding" designates a whole collection of capacities and abilities that go to make up the Christian life, and that inform the Christian reading of these texts. The collection and its configurations may be distinctively Christian, but its components are not exclusively Christian, since some of them are common to mature human existence generally, and all of them may be gained (if not mastered and ordered as fully as a lifetime of practice would permit) by non-Christians as well. Further, since the many competences that make up Christian understanding may vary individually in strength from person to person, it would be misleading to suggest that Christian understanding is something Christians "have" while others do not. We might say, however, that growth in Christian understanding is proper to Christian life, and that Christian understanding is strengthened by exercise.

What does Christian understanding comprise? It is sometimes supposed that the Christian message is a sort of hypothesis, which Christians "believe." That is what makes Christians Christians: their willingness to accept the hypothesis as a true one. On this model, Christian understanding might be depicted as that grasp of the hypothesis which would make a reasoned decision about it possible. One would have attained a Christian understanding when one had a clear view of the grounds and implications of the various historical and metaphysical claims involved in the Christian hypothesis, and of the way in which these claims are woven together into a unity. "Christianity" is, so to speak, the object to be understood.

What such a view tends to overlook or minimize is the fact that the Christian message presents a number of concepts whose mastery takes one in quite a different direction from that just indicated. One may set out to understand Christianity, only to find oneself confronted with the task of understanding oneself and one's world Christianly. And this may be a more arduous assignment than one had anticipated, particularly with regard to the self-understanding which is involved. What accounts for this unusual turn of events is that some of the concepts central to Christian teaching are rather complex, existentially rooted concepts whose acquisition entails particular kinds of moral and emotional growth. Such concepts as gratitude or joy have conceptual prerequisites, in that, for example, a capacity for gratitude presupposes a particular awareness of self and other, and a capacity for joy presupposes the capacity to care. So to learn these characteristically Christian concepts, and thus to "understand Christianity," involves one in what may be a fairly intensive and thoroughgoing education in human existence, particularly if one's education has been somewhat spotty up to this point. Lest this appear to exaggerate a commonplace, it is worth remarking that we are not born with these concepts, and that some of them appear to go against the ordinary human grain, despite the ordinariness of the terms associated with them, such as "faith," "hope," and "love." Theologically understood, faith, hope, and love are divine gifts, not to be reckoned as human achievements; yet the appropriation of these gifts, enabled by grace, just as clearly involves the development of the corresponding abilities, or clusters of abilities, which are then determinative of Christian life as lived "in the power of the Holy Spirit."

It implies no denial of the supposition that the Christian message also includes objective truth claims to recognize that the articulation of these claims also includes concepts whose acquisition has a subjective dimension. When Søren Kierkegaard wrote that "God is not a name but a concept,"[2] he was making the point that a right use of this basic term, which figures ultimately in all Christian claims about reality, takes more than an acknowledgment that "God" has a reference. Rather, an understanding of "God" relates to and affects one's understanding of everything else, one's own self in particular. In similar ways, if to a lesser extent, the concepts involved in, say, "creation," "incarnation," and "resurrection" are not simply elements of a Christian hypothesis or world view but are ingredient in Christian life itself.

It is because concepts such as these, whose mastery requires a certain self-development and self-qualification in the learner, figure so importantly in Christian scripture and tradition and in their appropriation by the Christian community that theological hermeneutics·must pay particular attention to the question of the conditions of Christian understanding. There is no denying that "the Bible can be understood like any other book" in that it is patient of many uses common to other writings and can be accurately described in terms appropriate to these uses—for example, as the literary remains of ancient religious groups, as writings disclosive of information about their times, or as products of the human mind which may yield insights into the workings of that mind. However, the Christian use of Christian texts involves a training no less focused and deliberate than the disciplines proper to these other uses, though quite different in character from some of them. Christian understanding of this material is not an ingenuous and haphazard exploitation of the texts, to be supplanted by these other, methodologically sophisticated and responsible approaches. It has its own integrity, durability, and discipline. It is not self-isolated from other approaches to the texts, and is in fact often enhanced by them. But it is not made superfluous by them. Although the Bible can be understood like any other book, not every understanding of it is a Christian understanding.

The older exegetical tradition of the church contained a number of directives to the interpreter seeking a Christian understanding of the text of scripture. Among them were directives concerning the interpreter's subjective disposition toward the texts (e.g., faith, prayer, humility), concerning the proper context of interpretation (e.g., in community, in dialogue with tradition, in accord with the *analogia fidei*), and concerning effective ways of listening to the text (e.g., as "Word of God," as pertaining to the Old or the New Covenant, as historical, prophetic, apostolic or evangelical utterance, as canonical or noncanonical text). Observations on these heads were embodied in many standard summaries of hermeneutical principles. With the rise of critical-historical exegesis and other nontraditional approaches to the biblical documents, many of these old directives were felt as strictures upon the free investigation of the texts and were quite understandably thrown off. These more recent studies have their own critical principles and procedures; they make their own requirements of the interpreter, they establish their own structures of accountability to standards and to colleagues, and they maintain their own ways of interrogating the material under study. It would be incongruous to expect of them an allegiance to the directives that have traditionally guided another sort of conversation with these texts.

It would show a similar confusion to dismiss these directives outright as of no value whatsoever. Whenever critical studies have had to struggle for a foothold against ecclesiastical opposition, the old hermeneutical principles have generally been misused as weapons against the innovators. The reputation of these principles has suffered accordingly, since their abuse by churchly authority only strengthens misapprehension as to their real point. To exhort an interpreter to humility, to a proper regard for tradition, and the rest, may not be simply a way of enforcing "agreement" (though, of course, such exhortations *can* have that intent and effect); it may instead be a way of aiding understanding, by bringing the reader into an appropriate relationship to the text, supplying examples of its use, calling attention to relevant context, and so on. Similarly, the designations traditionally given to scripture and its components can be viewed not simply as precritical, dogmatically inspired claims about the nature of these texts, but as hermeneutical clues as to how they may be Christianly understood. They suggest what the interpreter should listen for, or what relative weight and position should be given different elements of scripture.

Theological hermeneutics must consider carefully the functions served by these old directives. In the absence of ongoing reflection upon the conditions and the criteria pertinent to Christian understanding, interpretation in the church is bound to vacillate between a nostalgic imitation of the past and an assimilation of the principles and procedures of other interpretative disciplines. What is needed is not the repristination of a precritical exegetical style and its rules. Even if that were possible as a serious option, it would not be theological hermeneutics. As theological inquiry, theological hermeneutics is *critical* reflection upon Christian understanding. It asks not only how the aims and conditions of Christian understanding have been traditionally stated, but also whether and to what extent these statements are adequate. It asks not only what the Christian community has identified as the canon of its understanding and how that canon has functioned, but also whether that identification and use have properly served, and can continue to serve, to relate Christian understanding to its norm in Jesus Christ. In its normative and critical concerns, theological hermeneutics is inseparable from its context within the total discipline of theological reflection.

Christian theology is a critical inquiry into the truthfulness of Christian witness. To ask after the truthfulness of that witness is to ask two basic sorts of questions. First, is it truly Christian witness? That is, is this particular instance of Christian witness true to its own avowed intention to be Christian witness, and how well does it fulfill that intention in this situation? Secondly, is it true? To what general criteria of truthfulness is it accountable, and with what degree of clarity and cogency does it manifest its truth? These two dimensions of theological inquiry, though formally distinct, are inseparable in practice.

Theological hermeneutics pertains especially to the first of these dimensions. It aids the inquiry into the character of truly Christian witness by a continually renewed effort to determine what constitutes the Christian understanding of those texts upon which Christian witness depends; to identify and study the conditions and practices which enable that understanding; and to bring the endeavor of Christian understanding into proper relationship to its norm. These three elements—in brief, a concern for the aims, the conditions, and the canon of Christian understanding—comprise its distinctive task as a discipline of interpretation.

II
The Aims
of
Christian Understanding

Let us begin with a thesis: The principal aim of a Christian understanding of scripture, the aim which so embraces and orders all subsidiary aims that it may rightly be called *the* aim, is the knowledge of God. In an earlier age, the claim which this thesis advances might simply have been taken for granted, so that the statement of it would have been superfluous. Today it may seem superfluous for another reason: it would not occur to many interpreters to describe the goal of their efforts in this way. Not that they would necessarily deny the claim if it were proposed to them. They might well assent to it then as a proper theological statement of the eventual *telos* of exegetical labors from a Christian standpoint. That is, they might well grant that all scriptural interpretation in the church, of whatever sort, ought somehow to serve this end. But to grant the truth of the claim at some level of abstraction or at some stage of eschatological remoteness is one thing; to give it a place in one's ongoing reflections upon the practice of interpretation is another.

Too much should not be made of the fact that the term "the knowledge of God" is not particularly prominent in the current hermeneutical and exegetical vocabulary. That could be accounted for in several different ways. Terminology is not the issue. The point is rather that, for some substantial and deepgoing reasons, scriptural interpretation has lost touch with that understanding of its aim which our thesis represents. It will be necessary to identify and confront these reasons, since they are a significant part of our interpretative situation. But before doing so, we will give some attention to what is positively conveyed by the thesis, and particularly by that key term "the knowledge of God."

The opening sentence of John Calvin's *Institutes of the Christian Religion* runs: "Nearly all the wisdom we possess, that is to say, true and sound wisdom, consists of two parts: the knowledge of God and of ourselves."[3] It is clear that for Calvin these two parts are not two separate spheres of knowledge which might be pursued independently. They are the conjoint outcome of a single task. In the 1560 French version of the *Institutes*, Calvin states simply: "In knowing God, each of us also knows himself." The two are inseparably linked and interdependent. Self-awareness (particularly "of our own ignorance, vanity, poverty, infirmity, and— what is more—depravity and corruption") prepares us to know God; at the same time, a "clear knowledge" of ourselves, presumably even in respect of those qualities just mentioned, is unattainable apart from the knowledge of God. Furthermore, these two, knowledge of God and of ourselves, are not strictly isolable from our knowledge of the world. To know God and self aright involves knowing oneself precisely as a part of the whole of creation, of which one is a microcosm. It is to have an effective sense of one's proper relatedness to all creatures and to their creator. It is this knowledge which enables one to be who one is. There is thus no knowledge of God which is not appropriated in a life-shaping response, though that response may range from terror, flight, and denial to worship and obedience.

The theme of the knowledge of God is understandably a controlling factor in Calvin's theological writing. In this Calvin is not eccentric. Both in the central importance he assigns to the knowledge of God, and in his overall way of characterizing it, he is representative of the biblical and Christian traditions at large. The knowledge of God which these traditions generally commend is not, in the first instance, to be thought of as information about God which it is in one's interests to possess. To use the familiar distinction, it is not "knowledge about" but "knowledge of," not *savoir* but *connaître/connaissance* (for Calvin, *cognoissance*). It is a sustained personal awareness or existential apprehension of God, which profoundly determines one's existence.

That determination of existence is not, strictly speaking, a consequence of the knowledge. That is, the relationship between the knowledge of God and the existential determination is not adequately represented on the model of someone who, let us say, comes by the information that God exists, is just, and so forth, and in consequence of that information begins to live a different way. The relationship is rather more intrinsic. It is *through* the existential determination that one comes to know God, and to know God is to have one's existence determined in certain ways. Knowledge of God and effective self-knowledge grow together. One comes to know God by disposing oneself toward God in an appropriate fashion, which by the nature of the case also involves disposing oneself toward one's neighbor and the world in correspondingly appropriate ways. But at the same time, it is only in knowing God that one learns properly to dispose oneself toward God, neighbor, and world; and in learning that, one both learns and becomes who one is.

Of course, disposing oneself toward God does not produce knowledge of God as an assured result, as if it were some magical technique permitting one to know God at will. Nor on the other hand is the self-disposing properly understood as a sort of fixed and arbitrary prerequisite to knowledge of God, a trial whose completion is rewarded by divine self-revelation. Either of these distortions grossly misrepresents the actual relationship, and compromises the central Christian confession regarding the grace of God. It is important to avoid both while still recognizing the close interdependence of the knowledge of God and the self-knowledge by which one lives.

The common analogy with one's knowledge of another human being is useful. Here, too, a certain self-preparation and self-positioning is requisite as intrinsic to the relationship—if not at the bare outset, then certainly in its development—and has a considerable role in determining the character and extent of one's knowledge of another. Various concepts vital to selfhood and to personal relationships must be grasped, if not fully mastered, before one's knowledge of another will get very far. For instance, unless and until one has some understanding of such things as obligation, fidelity, and privacy, one's relationships are likely to be fairly restricted in scope and depth, and one's knowledge of others, as well as of oneself, quite meager. There are, moreover, some basic human capacities—for example, for trusting, valuing, hoping, rejoicing, and the like—whose absence or inhibition in oneself renders one incapable of knowing other persons insofar as these capacities figure in their lives. To what extent can I know a person whose life is formed around particular values or directed by a particular passion if I am simply unacquainted with those values or that passion myself? That person will forever be an enigma to me, our relationship a curiosity, unless I experience some growth. I need not come to share that person's values or passions, making them my own; but unless I come to understand what they are by extending my own capacities for valuing and caring and being moved, I will not

Over-reaching

Reductionistic

know the person whose own identity is so greatly affected by them.

But here the counterpart must also be acknowledged: At the same time that my knowledge of other persons depends upon my self-knowledge (and "self-knowledge" here means the mastery of those basic concepts through which I become a self, and the particular self I am), this self-knowledge is largely gained through my interaction with other persons. This does not mean that others tell me who I am, supplying me thus with a self along with my birth certificate or passport. It means that I become who I am by learning, in my experience with others, how to take possession of my abilities and capacities, how to affirm, order, refine, and direct them, how to modify and supplement them by participating in that common heritage of concepts which are not native to any of us alone, but through which, oddly enough, we have and exercise our individuality. Self-knowledge and knowledge of others are thus mutually conditioned and profoundly interdependent, and it is on this model that the relationship between the knowledge of God and self-knowledge may be understood. (For Calvin, apparently, the question "Which came first?" is as much out of place in this latter context as it seems to us in the former: there is no time at which a person is not related to God, nor aware—at some level of awareness, however slight or distorted—of that relationship.)

Kierkegaard's remark that "God is not a name but a concept" has already been cited. Its pertinence at this point should be evident, but it needs to be explored somewhat more. It rightly calls attention to the fact that coming to know God is not like being furnished with the name of an object which is ready to hand, or like being given a description of an object so that one will be able to recognize it should it appear. Much of our traditional God language makes this same point: God is objectively indescribable, and thus strictly unimaginable. Even the revealed name of God, as Karl Barth says, "consists in the refusal of a name."[4] Moses hears simply, "I AM WHO I AM" (Ex. 3:14). There is no way to deal with this God except directly, that is, by attending to God as and when God will be known. This means that coming to know God entails being given the capacities proper to that apprehension and that attentiveness. It is, in other words, a matter of conceptual growth; and that growth will be demonstrated (among other ways, to be sure) in the way one uses the concept "God."

To speak of the knowledge of God as a conceptual matter does not mean that "God is only a concept," in the reductionistic sense in which that claim is sometimes made, that is, that God is not "real." It does mean that the reality of God is different from the reality of objects which may be named and described. In order to discern the reality of God one must be given, not names and descriptions, but conceptual training. But this way of speaking also should not be taken to mean that to have the concept of God is to know God, for one may surely develop capacities and then fail to exercise them, for any number of reasons.

Concepts are instruments of understanding, opening up the possibility of new sorts of discernment and response. "Concept" itself is, as Ludwig Wittgenstein helpfully observes, a vague concept.[5] It would be unwise to give the use of the term too precise a delimitation. Generally speaking, a concept is a particular ability or capacity (or complex thereof), ordinarily related to language. That relation to language must not be narrowly understood, however. It is possible in some cases for someone to possess the abilities that make up a given conceptual competence without having the verbal facility that ordinarily is connected with it. On the other hand, a person may be quite familiar with the conventional use of a word or an expression, and to all appearances be able to use it correctly, and still lack the concept to which the expression is properly related—a fact which may, or may not, betray itself eventually. This is especially pertinent in cases where the concept in question has to do with a subjective disposition, perhaps difficult of attainment, while the corresponding word usage is pervasive and easily assimilated.

The inflation of our linguistic currency in this way is common: words are in abundant circulation with insufficient conceptual backing. In consequence, people may sometimes think they have a concept when in fact they are still far from it; or to put it another way, the concept they possess and the concept normally associated with the word may differ considerably. This latter way of putting the point may be more fortunate, since it is often difficult to specify what "having a concept" amounts to. For the having of some concepts there are clear and firm criteria; but for many, perhaps most, it is a question of degree. The extent of one's mastery of a concept is not indicated by the prominence of that concept in one's speech and behavior, but by the extent to which one can make ready and proper use of it on those occasions when its use is called for. (Knowing what those occasions are also belongs to one's conceptual mastery.)

Concepts differ in their existential significance. The presence or absence of some concepts in one's repertoire may make little difference to one's identity, character, and behavior. With others, the difference is momentous. Forgetting how to play chess, or how to parse a sentence in a foreign language, may have little effect on one's constitution and conduct; but forgetting the difference between right and wrong would be somewhat more serious, as Gilbert Ryle has observed—indeed, at such a different plane of seriousness that it seems absurd to speak of "forgetting" in this connection at all.[6] The distinction between right and wrong is an existentially fundamental distinction. Its loss would be bound up with a destructive transformation of selfhood. The loss or lack of a number of other concepts—for example, the ability to make various particular sorts of discriminating moral, aesthetic, or intellectual judgments—can have considerable existential import.

It seems absurd also to speak of forgetting God, yet this is a familiar theme in the Old Testament writings (e.g., Deuteronomy, Job, Jeremiah, Hosea, Psalms). It is clear from these usages that this forgetfulness really involves an orientation (or disorientation) away from the reality of God and thus away from the truth, with devastating consequences. And being reminded of God, coming to know God again, involves a thoroughgoing, often painful reeducation in human life and conduct. One cannot forget God and remain the person one has been; one cannot come to know God without having one's existence remolded in the knowing. The conceptual equipment involved in knowing God is of the most personal sort.

In fact, although Kierkegaard's remark is a helpful reminder, it may be well not to press too far the point that God is *a* concept. Knowing God involves the acquisition and exercise of a whole range of concepts. "The concept of God" encompasses and integrates a variety of capacities and abilities; that is, it comprises many concepts. It would even be unwise to presume too great a degree of perceptible integration among them. There is an important sense in which we never "have the concept" of God. We may apprehend, but never comprehend, God. We do not grasp the "essence" of God (to use Calvin's technical distinction, *quid sit Deus*), and thus attain mastery of the concept. But we may know what kind of God God is *(qualis sit)*.[7] Otherwise put, we may come to know, not what God is, but who God is; not God's nature, but God's identity. That knowledge is attained not by some sort of examination of God, but through relating to God in such ways that the conceptual capacities which permit that knowledge are implanted and developed in us. Among the concepts in question are some traditionally associated with the so-called attributes of God, the qualities that reveal who God is, such as God's holiness and righteousness, mercy and grace, freedom and faithfulness. Correlative to these are concepts that shape and permit human response to this sort of God, such as concepts of sin, contrition, worship, joy, and gratitude. Whether the primary apparent reference is to God or to human life, all these concepts are of the sort whose acquisition opens up new dimensions of human existence. Through them we are given new ways of attending to God and the world, and new ways of intending our lives. All of this is involved in the knowledge of God.

Our primary aim, as Christians, in the interpretation of scripture is to grow in that knowledge: to be reminded, against our inveterate tendency to forget, who God is and thus who we are, what God's bearing toward us is and what that means for our common life as God's creatures. Scripture serves this reminding function by disclosing God to us and simultaneously giving us the concepts requisite to our hearing and apprehending of that disclosure.

That last statement must immediately be qualified: Scripture *can* serve this function, when it is activated to do so. Scripture can be, and has been, understood in such a way as to make this possible. Exegesis can promote the knowledge of God. Whether it does so depends to a large extent upon the interpreter's readiness to use scripture to that end. That readiness involves more than willingness, and it can be thwarted by factors in the interpreter's situation which run counter to the interpreter's own intentions. One way of describing the chronic malaise of modern biblical interpretation is this: Knowing what we now know about the text, we simply cannot use it as our predecessors did. That this development has some overwhelmingly positive implications is undeniable, and should indeed be remembered and stressed at the first sign of longing for the good old days. But it has also made it quite difficult to relate either the practice of interpretation or hermeneutical discussion of that practice to that overall aim of a Christian understanding of scripture which our opening thesis sets forth.

The virtual atrophy of this understanding of the primary aim of interpretation is related to the changing fortunes of two other notions which, once conventional and functional, have become quite problematic. The first is the notion that the Bible is the Word of God—or, as it has sometimes been put, that God is the author of scripture. To read the Bible, at least if one is properly prepared and disposed toward the task, is, on this view, to be addressed by God. It is vital to remember in this connection that throughout most of Christian history, the declaration that the Bible is the Word of God has functioned not simply as a claim about the authority or the truth of scripture, but as a basic hermeneutical principle, informing the reader's understanding of the text. (Of the implications of that principle, more must be said.) Of course, the texts were generally acknowledged to have had human authors as well (God is *auctor primarius*), but this acknowledgment did not distract the reader from the central aim of listening to God's Word in the text. Indeed, an awareness of the human authorship ordinarily helped the reader understand the text, wherever terms, allusions, or usages needed to be explained in the light of the linguistic resources and conventions of a particular human author. The literal sense of the text, thus explicated as necessary, was to be read as the Word of God.

That idea of a "literal sense" of the text is the other venerable, yet currently problematic, notion to be mentioned. Although the precise definition and demarcation of *sensus literalis* varied from age to age and from interpreter to interpreter, it was generally held to be the plain sense of the text intended by God and comprehensible to a reader who, by participation in the community of faith, is furnished with the basic conventions governing its understanding. The reader need not perform any intricate critical operations upon the text (at least not in a self-conscious way), so as to wrest from it a meaning which it is reluctant to disclose. The literal sense is what the text says to a properly attentive reader; it is its obvious meaning. Of course, what is obvious to a reader depends a great deal on how the reader has been schooled to approach the text. "Literal sense" is intimately bound up with the conventions of reading, with the capacities and dispositions, linguistic and personal, which the reader brings to the text, by virtue of having been formed in a community with a fairly secure style of interaction with this material. In an essay sketching the history of the notion of "literal sense," Brevard S. Childs has traced its shifting contours in common and scholarly usage through the centuries, up to its eventual, and fatal, conflation with "original meaning" under the impact of the post-Enlightenment preoccupation with historical origins.[8] It is well to keep in mind how recent a development this latter usage of "literal sense" actually is, and to ponder its influence.

It is clear that neither the assumption that God is the author of scripture nor the assumption that God's Word subsists in the literal sense of the text was unchanging in its force or function throughout Christian history. Both assumptions have been articulated and defended in very different ways in different circumstances. Yet together, in whatever precise form, they have helped the users of scripture to read and hear it in ways which furthered their realization of that overall aim of Christian thought and life which is represented by the term "the knowledge of God."

How they serve that aim may be briefly suggested. To perceive the text as Word of God has profound hermeneutical consequences. The text then functions as an instrument through which God enters into a relationship with the reader. It is not simply a means whereby the reader learns what ancient writers and their sources thought about God. It is not even only a record of God's relationship with those ancient peoples. It is God's self-disclosure to the present reader or hearer. The narratives of the acts of God are then taken to have a certain point which might not be evident to someone who saw them primarily as history or as myth. As history, they appear to furnish putative information about past events, information that might or might not be corroborated by other accounts. As myth, they might set forth the self-understanding of their authors or show the significance their authors attached to particular events in their experience. But as Word of God, they disclose what sort of God it is with whom the reader or hearer has to do. The God whose identity is enacted according to these narratives, and enacted definitively in Jesus Christ, addresses the reader in these texts: "This is who I am for you."

To take the text as God's Word is to know who God is *pro me, pro nobis*. It is to be drawn into relationship with the one whose disclosure it is. The self-revelation of God can never be an incidental matter to any human being; to hear the Word of God is to be affected. This means that such a perception of the text influences not only the way one construes the text, important as that is, but the way one responds to it as well. Samuel Johnson's observation that "when a man knows he is to be hanged in a fortnight, it concentrates his mind wonderfully" has an analogue here.[9] One is moved by the actuality of God's self-disclosure in the text. It works an effect in the recipient. Because of this Word, one's world and one's self cannot be the same. This text must be lived. In the living of it, one's conceptual apparatus is developed and strengthened. The resources of the text are appropriated in response to the Word it con-

veys, so that one moves increasingly—to use Gerhard Ebeling's contrast—from "understanding *of* language" to "understanding *through* language,"[10] from a knowledge of the
text to the knowledge which the text fosters. Such knowledge does not leave the text behind, but the text comes into
use as the instrument rather than only the object of one's
knowing.

The activation of the text in this way is more readily
achieved when one approaches it not as a solitary reader
before an isolated text but as a member of a community in
which the text already has a life. The interpreter who first
hears the text as living voice, who witnesses that voice being
heard by others, and whose own identity is formed or re-
formed in interaction with those for whom this text is the
word of life, is in a different position from that of the interpreter who sits alone before a strange, mute document with
the task of teasing some meaning from it. To the first, the
text already says something; in its articulation and hearing
there has already been interpretation. But, more important
still, this interpreter has been given a way of using the text,
and has been initiated into the conceptual skills and capacities that mark an existence nourished on these writings.
The value of this sort of preparation is not so much that one
has been furnished an interpretation of the text—that can
be a mixed blessing indeed—but that one has been equipped
to make use of the text. Any received exposition always
needs to be rethought in the light of one's own continuing
experience with the text, unless the text is simply to become
the servant of the community in its program of socializa-
tion. But the interpreter who actually has the use of the text
may be in a far better position to hear the text afresh than
someone who comes to it without that sort of readiness.

Wittgenstein once compared philosophers to "savages,
primitive people, who hear the expressions of civilized men,
put a false interpretation on them, and then draw the queer-

est conclusions from it."[11] Anytime an expression is isolated from its ordinary use and is made the object of an inquiry in itself—a common procedure in philosophy at least since Plato—its separation from the conventions that govern its normal sense makes it uncommonly opaque. (In Wittgenstein's judgment, this accounts in part for the mystery we often associate with some of these philosophical targets, e.g., "being," "truth," "meaning.") The interpreter confronting an unfamiliar text apart from any community of interpretation is in a situation similar to that of the philosopher. To take the text "literally" under such circumstances —that is, to put an obvious construction upon it—may produce something quite remote from what the text's ordinary users might consider its literal sense. This literal sense—the "natural," "plain," "obvious" meaning which the community of faith has normally acknowledged as basic, regardless of whatever other constructions might also properly be put upon the text—is grounded in the community's own experience with the text. As those adjectives suggest, it is the sense whose discernment has become second nature to the members of the community. It is a grasp of this literal sense which permits one to understand through the text, rather than being forever preoccupied with the text itself. Along with the perception of scripture as Word of God, then, the notion of the literal sense of scripture has traditionally helped to sustain a reading of scripture which has as its primary aim the knowledge of God.

Both of these components of a conventional approach to scripture are in serious difficulty, not so much because of any direct attacks upon them as because of our increasing awareness of the human history of these texts. This is a familiar story by now, although the real dynamics of the process are still elusive and debatable. In some ways, these two notions led to their own and each other's dissolution. The vigorous exploration of the human origins of the bibli-

cal materials since the seventeenth century has often been
justified by Protestant exegetes as motivated by the aim of
recovering the literal sense of the documents—that is, what
the texts meant before they were smothered with an overlay
of dogmatic ecclesiastical interpretation. In the late nine-
teenth century, such interpreters as W. Robertson Smith
and William Newton Clarke still found it both proper and
effective to establish the credentials of their critical approach to scripture in this way; and their contemporary,
Frederic W. Farrar, in his 1885 Bampton Lectures could
still voice optimism that such scholarship, animated by
Christian love, would increasingly disclose the plain meaning of scripture by which Christian folk have always lived
despite the dogmas and theories of interpretation.[12]

A disconcerting result of these explorations has been the
discovery, from which Protestant theological exegesis has
not recovered, that the meaning of the texts in this sense is
anything but plain. Where, among the various layers of
tradition and amid the disparate oral and literary forms and
genres in scripture, is one to locate the literal sense of the
text? The main problem here is not the ambiguity of the
results of critical investigation, nor the fact that this sort of
interpretation demands special scholarly competence—
though both of these problems are serious enough, when
one considers their effect upon the notion of a stable literal
sense to which the community has ready access. But even
if the literary and preliterary history of the documents were
established beyond dispute and generally accessible, their
literal sense would not be evident; or to put it more accurately, the notion of "literal sense" itself has been rendered
inapplicable by the discovery of the varying functions per-
formed by the literary and linguistic forms in scripture.
What is the literal sense of myth, parable, apocalyptic, prophetic oracle? One may respond that the literal sense of
each is what it means. But while that immediately unil-

luminating response may be defensible, and indeed may be the shortest way to handle the query, it also eliminates from hermeneutical discussion the notion of literal sense as traditionally understood. The discussion of the aims of interpretation has shifted to new ground, leaving "literal sense" behind as an anachronism. The interpretation of scripture now embraces a number of specialized inquiries geared to the various sorts of material contained in or discernible beneath the texts of scripture. Each of these "genre specific" inquiries—for example, as to the proper interpretation of mythic or parabolic utterances—develops its own account of what it means to understand this particular sort of material. Alongside these specific inquiries, and occasionally interacting with them, various general strategies of reading such as structuralism have found a place; and these inquiries and strategies find their common basis for discussion, to the extent that they seek such a basis at all, in general or philosophical hermeneutics rather than in the Christian tradition of interpretation.

Among the consequences of this development has been the increasingly marked distancing of the business of interpretation from the community of faith as a whole. Particular members of the community may, of course, acquire these disciplines of interpretation for themselves, becoming knowledgeable in any or several of the exegetical specialties with their various fore-understandings, foundations, frameworks, and skills. Those who do not thus become specialists must be content to receive the interpretations and insights of those who do. But on neither side of this lay and professional distinction is there fostered the sort of mutual enhancement of textual understanding and personal growth which the old confrontation with and acquisition of the literal sense formerly produced. If we are all "laity," that is, dependent on the specialist and disqualified from any significant participation in discerning the sense of scripture ourselves, can we any longer be *laos,* the people of God? It seems clear enough, at any rate, that one of the principal ways the community has continually been nourished and constituted as *laos,* namely, through an ongoing active struggle with the text as instrument of God's self-disclosure, is threatened by the passivity which specialization engenders in the "laity."

At the same time that this earnest and errant pursuit of the literal sense of scripture was eroding the notion of literal sense itself, by another irony the conviction that the text was the Word of God was rendering interpreters incapable of reading the text as their ancestors, guided by that conviction, had read it. Hans W. Frei has given a fascinating account of this turn of events, which centered in the eighteenth century, in his *The Eclipse of Biblical Narrative.*[13] If scripture conveys the Word of God, it must be true. But the verisimilitude of much of scripture as conventionally read was seriously called into question by modern developments both in our understanding of the world of nature and history and in our understanding of human thought and language. Interpreters who wished to preserve the truth of scripture then found themselves forced to choose between a defense of the conventional reading against modernity (a defense which, because it still saw the issue in modern terms, subtly undercut the position it was intended to support), and an unconventional reading which would relocate the truth value of scripture. In taking the latter option, interpreters could choose among several alternatives, the most successful of which represented the texts as the poetic efforts of human beings to express their consciousness of, or their experience of, the divine. On this view, it becomes important then to trace the development of these expressions and to find ways to recover the original form of consciousness, the original experience, or the original historical event which has come to expression in the text.

But when this route is taken, something happens to that description of the text as "Word of God." If it is not explained (and dismissed) as simply a time-honored way of pointing to the religious significance of the text, sharing the text's poetic mode of expression, at any rate it can hardly be applied straightforwardly to the text any longer. It has ceased to have a positive hermeneutical function, and can only be affirmed, if at all, in a carefully qualified sense. And so by a strange development, the assumption that scripture is to be read and heard as the Word of God led to an effort to vindicate the truth of scripture, which resulted in the enervation of the assumption itself and to its elimination as a functioning hermeneutical principle.

Furthermore, when attention is shifted from the text itself to the mode of consciousness, experience, or historical event which is taken to have triggered the process leading to the text's production, one result is a decided loss of interest in the literal sense of the text. It is not the verbal sense conveyed by the text itself, but rather what is behind or within the text, which is of greatest significance. This has implications not only for how one reads the text but also for how one envisions its authority and function as canon, and it has led, quite understandably, to some interesting proposals for relocating the canon.[14]

Of course, there were crises, clashes, and incongruities in the application of these two notions prior to this great modern transformation. From early in the church's history, for example, there have been occasions when the affirmation that God is the author of scripture has led to a denigration of its literal sense—either because God simply could not have meant what the text obviously says or because the interpreter has discovered an alternate way of reading the text which yields meanings so profound or so ripe with possibilities that they must be from God. The tension between these two notions, as well as within them, has always been there to complicate the Christian use of scripture. The chief cause of problems is solutions.

Moreover, scriptural exegesis guided by these notions has carried with it liabilities far beyond those immediately perceived by the exegete or the community. Under some form of the conviction that the Bible in its literal sense is the Word of God, slavery and exploitation have been sanctioned, holy wars promoted, patriarchal societies upheld, knowledge suppressed, cruelty institutionalized. We cannot for a moment seriously regret the passing of these notions, when we remember and still witness their human cost. And no sanction should be given to their rehabilitation, or to the rehabilitation of the approach to scripture which they sustain, unless that rehabilitation incorporates some substantial revisions and critical safeguards.

It is just such critical revision which is proposed in what follows. Having suggested how the primary aim of a Christian understanding of scripture may be described, the task that remains is to establish an approach to the use of scripture by which that aim may be realized. This entails the ensuring of the exercise of critical reflection upon every aspect of scripture and its interpretation. That is, the realization of this aim not only permits but demands the exercise of reasoned judgment upon the contents of scripture and upon the results of its interpretation, in the light of God's self-disclosure. Christian understanding can still be nourished by the literal sense of scripture, hearing in it the Word of God. But this cannot be accomplished by a retreat into the past, or by the steadfast exclusion of the problems and possibilities which are the contemporary exegetical heritage. It will require rather more versatility in the use of scripture, more readiness for personal involvement, and more critical discernment than we may wish. But such, in our time, is the path of what H. Richard Niebuhr called "the never-ending pilgrim's progress of the reasoning Christian heart."[15] It is time for a fuller description of that path.

III
The Conditions
of
Christian Understanding

A pair of disclaimers at the outset should help to clarify the purpose of this phase of hermeneutical reflection. First, what follows is not an overview of exegetical method. Neither is it a substitute for careful attention to questions of exegetical method, as if one could use hermeneutics to overleap such practical considerations and gain an immediate understanding of a text. Hermeneutical reflection does not replace exegetical discipline. Its purpose is, rather, to make explicit and to pursue some considerations that should precede and accompany the adoption, refinement, and use of exegetical skills. A grasp of the aims and conditions of a Christian understanding of scripture should help an interpreter to determine whether and how a particular exegetical technique may contribute to its realization, and to bring both exegetical and personal resources appropriately to bear upon the interpretative task.

Secondly, the following considerations do not belong to a transcendental inquiry into the *a priori* conditions of human understanding. This disclaimer would be gratuitous if hermeneutics had not come to be generally identified with that sort of inquiry over the last century and a half. In the laudable desire to make hermeneutics a reflective discipline of interpretation rather than the mere assembly and transmission of practical rules of thumb, Friedrich Schleiermacher and his successors turned their attention to the phenomenon of understanding as such. Once we know what understanding really is and how it happens, they reasoned, we will be able to evaluate procedures and recommend interpretative techniques which will produce understanding in our handling of texts. General hermeneutics in its major representatives has since become an effort to give an adequate account (theory, phenomenology, or ontology) of the process or event of understanding. (The language descriptive of the character of the account sought, as well as of its object, has varied as the inquiry has progressed.) These representatives have been unified in the conviction that "understanding" denotes a describable phenomenon and that the most effective way to grasp that phenomenon is to set out "the conditions of its possibility," to use the Kantian phrase.[16]

The present investigation of the conditions of Christian understanding turns on quite a different supposition, namely, that "understanding" is less aptly characterized as *phenomenon* than as *ability*—to the extent that any general characterization of it may succeed. This supposition has already been disclosed in Chapter I, and was operative in the discussion of "concepts" in the second. A somewhat fuller account of this approach to the use of the term "understanding," and of its more particular import in the phrase "Christian understanding," will clarify what a treatment of the conditions of that understanding will involve.

There is at least some *prima facie* evidence to support the supposition that "understanding" is most profitably treated in terms of capabilities.[17] When you are trying to ascertain whether or to what extent I understand something, ordinarily you would be ill-advised to accept, as definitive evidence of my understanding, such things as my avowals of certainty about my understanding, my account of its profundity, my narrative of the way the understanding came to me, or my description of what it feels like to understand. To be sure, the acquisition and possession of understanding will often be associated with such experiences and convictions, and in certain cases it would be reasonable to doubt whether I understand if I offer none of these signs, just as it is reasonable to doubt the presence of a disease if none of its common symptoms are in evidence. Still, understanding does not consist in the presence of these signs, nor are they strictly a part of its definition. To gauge the accuracy or depth of my understanding, you will, if you are careful, want to see how I perform with it, and see what difference my supposed understanding makes under relevant circumstances. However impressive the phenomena associated with my understanding may be, the confidence their presence may have inspired in you (and in me) will, and should, quickly evaporate if I blunder in every attempt to operate with my understanding, or if I simply fail to utilize it when a situation calls for it.

Of course, what you will count as evidence of my understanding depends upon the situation—not only upon the object of my understanding (the poem, the law, the request), but also upon the context which your examination presupposes as relevant. If you are wondering whether I have understood an incident in the play we are watching, you may be wondering, for instance, whether my grasp of idiomatic English is sufficient for me to follow the actors' conversation, or whether I have seen how this incident contributes to the plot, or whether I have caught the veiled reference to contemporary political events. And my response to your query may well reveal that I understand in some respects but perhaps not in others.

Because of the great variety of situations within which "understanding" has application, it is not very helpful to begin an inquiry into the conditions of understanding with the question which, to some, has seemed the obvious starting point: What does it mean to understand anything at all? To pursue the inquiry along this line inevitably leads to the adoption of some single strong paradigm for "understanding," probably borrowed from a field of inquiry where it has proven effective, and broadened for universal applicability. About this approach two things must be said. First, it is obvious that in one sense a good many such paradigms have very far-reaching (if not strictly universal) applicability: that is, a particular kind of inquiry may range far and wide for its subject matter, bringing all sorts of material under its scrutiny. There can be no objection in principle to this procedure. One may rightly seek a historical understanding of a religious text, or a physiological understanding of human behavior, or a psychological understanding of an occurrence in history—despite the fact that these may not, at the time, be the normal or conventional ways to approach the subject in question. Many an important development has begun when a discipline of inquiry has ventured beyond its conventional subject-matter boundaries onto turf occupied by the practitioners of another sort of interpretation, bringing a new illumination to the territory.

But secondly, we must acknowledge the strong temptation to universalize the *principles* of an inquiry, or, to put it another way, to insist that this sort of inquiry should supplant all other treatments of the subject matter, especially when the inquiry has shown impressive new results. Even while we recognize and affirm the value of extending the range of our various disciplines of inquiry ever more fully, it is vital to retain the adjective or adverb qualifying the inquiry in each case: "*historical* understanding," "interpreting *psychologically.*" The qualifier reminds us of the particularity of the aims and criteria of the inquiry; it reminds us that there is no understanding in general, of which every

achieved understanding is an instance. Several fields of inquiry may of course have some common criteria for "understanding," so that a shared paradigm might be abstracted
from their accounts. But it is well to remember that this is
an abstraction, not a foundation. "Understanding" is context-dependent not merely in its more remote outworkings
but at its center: what it means to understand, and how that
understanding may be achieved, vary enormously, so that
it is imperative to begin with the particular situation, and
not with a general overview; to ask, not, What is the nature
of understanding, and how is it possible? but rather, What
counts as understanding in this case, and how is that understanding gained?

The sign says, "Keep off the grass." Do I understand it?
You ask me what it means, and I restate the injunction for
you in one or two appropriate ways, and even offer the
equivalent in Spanish. So far, so good; I seem to understand
the sign. I then proceed to walk across the lawn upon which
the sign is posted. Have I failed to understand the sign after
all? Not necessarily: understanding does not entail assent or
obedience. So you test me further: "What are you doing?
The sign says, 'Keep off the grass'!" At this point I can offer
you any of various indications that I realize that I am (or
seem to be) disobeying the sign, perhaps coupled with some
explanation for my contrary behavior: "Someone moved
the sign; it belongs over there," or "I know, but I'm in a
hurry," or "So arrest me!" But if I respond instead with a
blank stare, betraying no awareness of the relationship between the sign and my behavior, do I understand the sign?
Despite my facility in paraphrasing, explaining, and trans-
lating the message, you would be justified in concluding
that I do not. You might say that I appear to understand the
words, but that somehow I have missed the point. Or you
could say that I can tell you what the sign means, but that
I have not grasped its significance.

The point; the significance (i.e., what the sign "signifies"): some of the common terms for what it is that I have missed suggest, superficially, that the way to move beyond word understanding to real understanding is to discover what the words point to. Even when the primitive notion that words are essentially signs for things has been discarded, this referential view of language is apt to linger, manifesting itself again in ever-renewed attempts to correlate language and reality, to draw connecting lines between—if not word and thing—expression and experience, linguistic form and subject matter. This notion may even lead someone to speak as though the main business of a poem or a story were to refer, if not directly then obliquely, if not to actual or possible features of the external world, then to the inner states or feelings of the poet or narrator. Given this assumption, one might readily believe that in order to understand an utterance the main thing is to find that to which the utterance refers.

Yet to introduce the notion of reference as a way of explaining my failure to understand the sign is surely to introduce a major problem. Not that it would take any ingenuity to do so—for example, by saying that the difficulty was my failure to note that the sign "referred" to me, or to this lawn, or to the situation. (Would the mistake have been prevented if the sign also read, "This means you!"?) The problem with this is that although the message the sign carries obviously involves reference to its context, the point of the sign is not to refer. It is not, strictly speaking, a sign, functioning to stand for something. Now, one might say that the sign stands for the warning the grounds keeper would give me in person, if present. And that personal word of warning, of course, signifies the grounds keeper's wish that we would stay off the grass. One might say that —but it is doubtful that one would be inclined to say it if one were not under the necessity of vindicating a referen-

tial view of language, for it is a decidedly inelegant procedure, involving as it does the invocation of a grounds keeper
and a grounds keeper's wish and still falling short of its aim.

My lack of understanding cannot be attributed to my
failure to discern behind the sign a grounds keeper's wish,
since I could as easily fail to comprehend the wish as the
sign, even if I did discern it. (How does one discern a wish?
A moment's reflection on that question should yield an
awareness of the limits of any model which posits wishes
and similar mental phenomena as objects which their expressions, oral or written, signify.) No, the "point" of the
sign is not to point, either to its reader or to the situation
or to the hypothetical wishes of its sponsor. Its point is,
rather, its function in a given context. My failure with
regard to the sign is not a failure to note its reference, but
a failure to grasp its use. I have somehow fallen short of a
sufficient grasp of the conventions governing the use of
"Keep off the grass" signs to know how to respond to them
—or at least to this one. Despite my understanding of the
words I lack the conceptual mastery such signs depend
upon for whatever effectiveness they have. Without further
exploration of this situation it is impossible to tell just what
the problem is, since there are innumerable ways in which
something can be misunderstood.

The sign is an instrument employed for a specific purpose; and proper attention to it requires, in addition to
verbal understanding, a grasp of its function in the situation. That in turn requires both a familiarity with the ordinary use of "Keep off the grass" signs and the ability to
apply that knowledge to the particular features of the situation. My response to the sign's presence in a shop window,
in the weed-grown yard of an abandoned house, or on a
dormitory wall will differ from my response to its presence
on a tended lawn, insofar as I recognize the latter as the
context of the ordinary use of such signs while in the for-

mer instances the ordinary use is, I suspect, suspended or qualified in some way. And of course, since the situation is not simply what I find but what I create in part by my presence, that too must figure in my response: I may, for instance, judge (rightly or wrongly) that the ordinary use of the sign does not or should not apply to me or to this instance. When I start across the lawn and you call me to account, I may indicate to you through my reply that I understand the sign but that I have assessed the situation and decided to disregard it. You may then judge that I have understood the sign and misunderstood the situation, or that I have understood both sign and situation and still acted wrongly, or that my action is justifiable.

Three components of this incident are worth remarking. An "understanding" response to the sign seems to require: (1) a grasp of the verbal sense of the sign; (2) the possession of the concepts pertinent to the ordinary employment of such signs; (3) an ability to judge whether this particular context is one in which the ordinary use of the sign does and should apply. Though these are distinguishable elements, they are not best thought of as successive stages or isolable phases of understanding. They are normally closely interrelated, interdependent, often even simultaneously achieved abilities. The interdependence of a mastery of the verbal sense of a text and the conceptual growth proper to its employment may be far clearer, as well as more complete, in some other cases than it is in the present one. In getting the point of a joke, or in following a story, the two may be inseparable, since each of these may require an investment of our own experience—or a willingness to entertain new experience. In his treatment of historical understanding, W. B. Gallie has remarked that "stories are one of the main means by which a child is taught to 'have feelings' in characteristically human ways: that is, feelings for and with other human beings and for himself *as* a human being."[18] A story may function for us, when we understand it, differently from the way this sign functions for us: in the story, the verbal sense can be the vehicle of conceptual exercise and growth, while the sign is normally only an occasion for the exercise of abilities which must be presupposed. A fuller treatment of this complex relationship between what has here been called "verbal" and "conceptual" understanding awaits.

Whether the third component, applicatory judgment, properly belongs to the understanding of the sign is debatable, and it is easy enough to see why. In one sense, understanding is independent of "application." That is, it is possible that I have understood "Keep off the grass" signs for years before actually encountering my first one (say, if I have spent my childhood in the desert). It would be ludicrous to say that I began understanding the sign only upon that first encounter. On the other hand, if I manifest a total inability to recognize a situation to which the sign applies when I do encounter one, it is obvious that I do not understand the sign—insofar as understanding the sign involves understanding its use. Understanding, or its lack, is *demonstrated* in application; and the ability to make judgments pertinent to application is a part of understanding, although the application itself is not. "There is no understanding without application" overstates the connection. "There is no understanding without the ability to apply" is preferable.

But this last point must not be misconstrued. There may well be cases in which the only *route* to understanding is some sort of "application," at least of a provisional sort— that is, a concrete effort to deal with a situation in terms of what one is trying to understand. One learns to judge painting, it may be, by judging painting in company with other, more skilled judges who will help. Without direct engagement, the abilities will not develop. This may indeed be more nearly the rule than the exception, so far as the attainment of new concepts is concerned. But it is still important to distinguish the understanding, once attained, both from the "applications" through which it was formed and from the "applications" to which it may be put, simply in the interests of clarity. As the history of the use of Isa. 7:9 ("Unless you believe, surely you will not understand"[19]) demonstrates, such clarity may be crucial.

The incident discussed here illustrates understanding of a particular, context-dependent sort, bound to a context in which the sign is functioning conventionally and where the question at issue was whether I understood it in its function. A person might attend to the sign in many other ways —for example, as a cultural artifact: examining the orthography, the paint, etc., for evidence as to the sign's origin, or considering what the sign reveals about the values and ways of the culture which produced and used it. A member of another culture—a grassless society, say, or one in which lawns are intended as public thoroughfares—might even experience a modest *Horizontverschmelzung* upon confronting this sign, as the product of one culture illuminates and, however subtly, affects the course of another. In such instances, the sign is being made instrumental to different sorts of understanding from that previously considered in the context of ordinary use. The explication of its verbal sense, the acquisition of familiarity with its ordinary use, and data concerning this particular sign in this particular setting may all enhance this "artifactual" understanding; but they do not exhaust its scope, nor are they all always pertinent to the attainment of a particular purpose in such an inquiry, as the advocates of various interpretative approaches make clear when they rule one or another sort of consideration irrelevant to their aims.

It is just as obvious that the sign may be used in numerous other ways which have little or nothing to do with

either its customary use or its verbal sense. Verbal sense
may be given a new twist when the sign is put into play as
a warning against marijuana (here, the literal sense is su-
perseded); it may be disregarded altogether when the sign
is posted on the lawn as a prearranged signal that the
coast is clear. (The difference between the two cases is evident: "Keep off the grass" may mean "Abstain from marijuana," in current vernacular American; it cannot mean
"The coast is clear." The first use depends for its success
upon a reader's making the appropriate connections in the
context, while the second use cannot presuppose any
connection that has not been explicitly established by the
parties involved.)

This illustration has not been explored at such length
with the intention of establishing a paradigm for the Christian understanding of scripture. The illustration is of restricted applicability to that enterprise. But it does have
some bearing on it. Central to this hermeneutical inquiry is
the thesis that scripture, Christianly understood, is instrumental to the knowledge of God; and so it was useful (as will
be evident later) to consider a small "text" which is clearly
an *instrument* in its primary context, rather than, say, an
object of inquiry or of contemplation. The three elements
comprising the understanding of that instrument—verbal
explication, conceptual mastery, applicative judgment—
may be readily identified as components of the Christian
understanding of scripture, and indeed correspond at least
to one reading of the classic threefold pattern of theological
exegesis: *explicatio, meditatio, applicatio.* [20] The illustration is
less apt, however, when it comes to a determination of the
specific character and interrelationships of those three elements in Christian understanding. It provides a simple reference point for the task of developing—partly by comparison, partly by contrast—a more direct account of the
conditions of Christian understanding.

Let us begin with a look at a classic master of a strictly explicative approach to hermeneutics. Johann August Ernesti's *Institutio interpretis Novi Testamenti*, first published in 1761, enjoyed more than half a century of prominence as a practical hermeneutical manual. An English version by Moses Stuart of Andover, *Elements of Interpretation*, went through several editions from 1822 onward, extending Ernesti's influence in America and England even while it was on the wane in his native Germany. For Ernesti, the key to the interpretation of biblical as well as any other material is the establishment and mastery of the *usus loquendi*, the use which the speakers or writers make of their words. Verbal sense depends upon the *usus loquendi*, "because the sense of words is conventional and regulated wholly by usage. Usage then being understood, the sense of words is of course understood."[21] This does not mean that the sense of an utterance is wholly determined by standard linguistic conventions; each writer has a style, a personal *usus loquendi*, which is the writer's own appropriation and modification of the available language. But one can determine the sense of an utterance only by immersing oneself first in the linguistic usage of the writer's place and time, and then in the writer's own characteristic usage insofar as that can be determined. This requires an acquaintance with particular historical circumstances as well as with the general grammatical and lexical features of the language. The aim is to establish the literal sense of the utterance, the sense which common usage and context would have rendered obvious to the writer's public, unless there are clear indications that a nonliteral or "tropical" sense is intended; and even then, the trope is to be interpreted "grammatically," that is, on the basis of the linguistic evidence as to how it should be construed.

Ernesti was well aware that verbal sense is not always

clear and unambiguous even when one is familiar with ordinary usage. He acknowledged that one may have to appeal to indirect evidence to establish meaning: primarily, to what one may gather of the author's purpose or scope in the discourse in question, but also to various sorts of analogies with material that one takes to be similar, and even finally (and still more cautiously), to common sense and ordinary experience. Ernesti granted, then, that the use of words in a given instance cannot always be discerned on the basis of "usage": an author has a certain freedom in this regard, though that freedom should not be exaggerated since the author who strays too far from convention will simply be unintelligible. Where usage is ambiguous, or has been violated, or is unknown to the interpreter, indirect testimony may provide some clues. But this is only a resort for an interpreter who has been baffled in the ordinary pursuit of sense by way of the ordinary study of the *usus loquendi.* Ernesti is adamant that interpretation should never begin anywhere other than with the words of the text and with the attempt to establish their sense. And he is equally clear that the work of the interpreter strictly ends with the establishment of verbal sense. "It is by the *words* of the Holy Spirit only that we are led to understand what we ought to think regarding *things.* Said Melanchthon very truly: 'The Scripture cannot be understood *theologically,* until it is understood *grammatically.*' "[22]

In a distinction that has become mildly notorious, Ernesti stated that two requisites of a competent interpreter were *subtilitas intelligendi* and *subtilitas explicandi* (as rendered by Stuart, "an acute understanding" and "acuteness or skill in explanation"). By the first, which embraces all the skills for determining the *usus loquendi,* the interpreter discerns the sense of a passage. By the second, the interpreter exhibits that sense precisely and clearly in language accessible to the interpreter's own public. Hermeneutics is, then, "the science which teaches to find, in an accurate and judicious manner, the meaning of an author, and appropriately to explain it to others."[23]

In his earliest extant notes on hermeneutics, Schleiermacher accepts this distinction but declares that only the *subtilitas intelligendi* "genuinely belongs to hermeneutics. As soon as the *subtilitas explicandi* becomes more than the outer side of understanding, it becomes part of the art of presentation, and is itself subject to hermeneutics."[24] Schleiermacher was doubtless correct both in noting that the "presentation" of a text in a useful rerendering or commentary may involve skills and considerations beyond those requisite to one's own grasp of a text and in perceiving that such a presentation is itself a proper object of further interpretation. No one engaged in the public exposition of texts, or in reading previous expositions, would want to quarrel fundamentally with these observations. (It is, of course, also undeniable that one often comes to a better understanding of a text by trying to explain it to others, so the distinction should not be overdrawn.) Yet Schleiermacher's exclusion of *subtilitas explicandi* from the discipline of understanding (except as "the outer side of understanding") is misleading insofar as it encourages the impression that real understanding is something like an intuitive inward grasp of the object, while discursive explication is only the shadow or husk or contingent outcome of this event. Schleiermacher would not have countenanced such a drastic separation himself, as his own continued efforts to maintain the relationship between "subjective" and "objective," "grammatical" and "psychological" components in interpretation demonstrate. But his adaptation of Ernesti's distinction certainly encouraged a growing tendency in hermeneutics to subordinate the grammatical to other considerations in the search for the meaning of a text.

Ernesti's own choice of the terms of his distinction seems

unfortunate in retrospect. It is clear from his own explanation and use of the terms that he does not associate *subtilitas
intelligendi* with the intuitive and subjective at the expense
of the discursive and contextual. The accent is, rather, on
the latter, since it is only through a mastery of the grammar,
the *usus loquendi*, and the particular circumstances of an
utterance that one may perceive what the words signify.
The subjective dimension in interpretation comes in for
very little positive attention in his manual; although it is
surely implied throughout, inasmuch as gaining mastery of
verbal usage involves learning and growth of one sort or
another, Ernesti simply devoted his attention to delineating
the objective task of explicating the verbal sense of a text.
We shall need to give fuller attention than he did to the
growth of understanding as a matter affecting the interpreter's own self. But it would be a serious mistake to con-
centrate on this aspect apart from a consideration of its
relationship to the explication of verbal sense. In other
words, the positive role of explication in textual understanding, and thus in the understanding of discourse generally and Christian discourse in particular, needs to be
affirmed and developed. Although it may be quite in order
to identify the "art of presentation" as a separate task, either
within the scope of hermeneutics as Ernesti has it, or, as
Schleiermacher locates it, beyond the scope of hermeneutics proper, it is vital to give due weight to the function of
explication as a means of understanding. Explication is not
just something that follows upon understanding, either as
a means of solidifying it or as a means of communicating it
to others. We explicate a text first to ourselves in order to
understand it. It is through explication that one comes to
understand verbal sense in the first place.

Ernesti indicates why this is so, when he reminds us that
the connection between words and meaning is not "natural
and necessary," but conventional.[25] (In his own way of de-

veloping this point, Ernesti seems quaintly Lockean; but this basic insight, at least, is not outdated.[26]) It is through usage that words have sense, and consequently a large part of interpretation is the establishment and mastery of the usage in question so that the words may be rightly understood. The interpreter must participate, at least in a provisional way, in the *usus loquendi* in order to grasp the sense. When the sense *seems* natural and necessary, it is because we do in fact participate in that usage: the words fit some single, unambiguous usage which is already ingrained in us, while no likely alternative has appeared on our mental horizon. But it is nonetheless true that even in such a case we have taken the words in one way and not in another. And it is likely that we have been helped, however unbeknownst, in our doing so by an awareness of the context, or by our own interests and circumstances, as well as by our general familiarity with the ordinary range and variety of uses of the expressions in question. We have in fact explicated the utterance to ourselves; or, if that seems too large a claim ("explication" suggesting too much of a full-scale, formal effort), we have at least construed the words, putting a construction upon them, making something of them, which we believe or assume to be justified. Explication in the fuller sense is only a more reflective, often more detailed performance of the same operation which is fundamental to any grasp of verbal sense.

A detailed treatment of explicative technique as such would be out of place here, and largely redundant besides. Practitioners of the methods of critical-historical exegesis which have developed since Ernesti's day (and to which his own advocacy of a strictly philological, nondogmatic exegesis of scripture gave impetus) have in large part been devoted to the recovery of the *usus loquendi* of the biblical material, and in their expositions of this material have, on the whole, taken the route of what the literary scholar E. D.

Hirsch, Jr., calls the "process of validation," testing their constructions of sense on the basis of the textual and historical evidence established.[27] The congruence of this procedure with Ernesti's basic principles is apparent. Of course, Ernesti did not realize the extent to which the search for the *usus loquendi* would complicate biblical interpretation by revealing the multitude of sources and authors behind the scriptural texts and the great diversity of linguistic forms and functions they embrace. The task of locating each particular element of tradition and describing its character, provenance, and context has often proved so overwhelming, and its theological value so obscure, that the fuller task of explication has been neglected in favor of a strictly historical study of the material, followed perhaps by an attempt to explain its significance.

For Ernesti, however, the significance of the text would be disclosed only through the patient explication of its verbal sense. He could hold interpretation strictly to this explicative task because he understood the texts in their canonical form to be written "by men divinely inspired" and therefore, in a primary sense, to be of divine authorship. He inferred from this also that one may take the Bible as one coherent record, containing no real contradictions, and interpretable in terms of itself, that is, the clearer portions illuminating the less clear.[28] Later followers of his philological method were led in part by it to doubt the accepted accounts of the authorship of the biblical writings and to discover an unexpected and bewildering array of viewpoints in the material; they could no longer affirm the essential simplicity and coherence of scripture, and the issue of inspiration or divine authorship became ever more problematic. If meaning is to be determined by the *usus loquendi,* and if the usage in question is that of the historical human authors of the material (as Ernesti himself stipulated), what alternative does one have?

There is, however, an alternate approach to the question of authorship, and thus to the determination of the *usus loquendi*, which may overcome this difficulty in Ernesti's hermeneutics: We may turn his assumption into an explicit decision. That is, where Ernesti *assumed* that the words of the scriptural text may be explicated coherently as the Word of God, we may *decide* to take them so. He assumed this because he was convinced of the inspired authorship and the basic consistency of the biblical writings, and had not been troubled with a disturbing awareness of their actual development in all their distinctive variety. We may decide to take them as the Word of God, even with our own knowledge of what they are as human documents. The fact that this is a decision and not a finding in disregard of historical evidence should be emphasized. Though in another sense it may be a finding—that is, our decision may be a concurrence in the church's confession that the Word of God is indeed to be heard in these texts—it is not a finding based on the historical examination of the circumstances of the origin and development of the biblical material. Inspiration is not a historical category. Whether a text is able to function as the Word of God cannot be established or denied through a study of its human genesis. If an interpreter takes it as such, or, more properly put, takes it as a text that may function as God's Word, this is a hermeneutical decision and should be acknowledged accordingly.

Whether and how such a decision may be justifiable is a question whose fuller consideration properly belongs to an examination of the authority of scripture. That such a decision is *possible*, however, should be obvious. The fact that an utterance has a specifiable author does not exclude its being used by another author, and thereby becoming, in some respects at least, another instance of discourse. Large parts of John Wesley's *Explanatory Notes Upon the New Testament* are borrowed directly (with an ingenuous acknowledgment) from J. A. Bengel's *Gnomon Novi Testamenti* and from other works; yet it is entirely proper to read Wesley's *Notes* as Wesley's work, inasmuch as in it he said what he wanted to say, albeit through the words of others. Such a practice in authorship was much more common in the ancient world, which may be one reason that the notion that the human words of scripture could also be God's utterance occasioned little consternation.

There is a notable difference (considerations of plagiarism aside; authorship is being viewed here in a less restricted sense) between quoting or citing the words of another and appropriating them as one's own utterance. An understanding of this difference is crucial to an understanding of what it means to take a human utterance as the Word of God. An author may quote the work of another in order to criticize or praise it, or to support an argument with it, or simply to remind the reader of it; but even if the author agrees wholeheartedly with the quoted material, it remains the work of its original author and has not yet become an utterance for which the one who is quoting assumes authorship. To assume authorship, to make the words one's own, changes their status and function, at least potentially. For instance, if I am watching a baseball game and at one point I inform a runner, "You're out!" my expression of opinion has no official status within the game. If an umpire an instant later repeats my very words, they have a different effect. With those words the umpire is authorized to perform a function which I cannot. If the umpire were clearly quoting my words ("He says you're out!") and not appropriating them, the quotation would be irrelevant and probably confusing. Again, if I draft a resolution which a deliberative body later enacts, my words have a different function afterward from the one they would have had if they simply appeared in the minutes as a proposal.

Moreover, in this latter case the words enter a new interpretative context: I may have intended the resolution to be taken in one way, while the enacting body may take it in another. In the context of that body's other utterances and ongoing policy the resolution may assume quite a different force from my intention. It has become the utterance of the body, and as such it is to be interpreted in the light of the body's usages. This is not to say that the utterance can no longer mean what I took it to mean. Obviously it can have both meanings. What its interpreter must determine at the outset is whose use of it is at issue, and thus what the relevant context of interpretation may be. What the utterance means as my proposal may differ considerably from what it means as the official statement or policy of the group. It is preferable to regard this as a change in meaning rather than only as a change in the "significance" of an utterance whose meaning remains stable. There has in effect been a change in authorship; and with it a change in what Ernesti called the *usus loquendi*, upon which the determination of meaning depends.

Similarly, a pericope common to two or three of the Synoptic Gospels may conceivably have a different meaning in each, since it has been assumed into a different authorship in each. Additionally, of course, it may have still another meaning in its original context, if it antedates all three Gospels. These meanings need not be widely disparate; the differences may be subtle or pronounced. Finally, the meaning of the pericope may be transformed again if one holds (as precritical interpretation often did) that in some sense the biblical canon as a whole provides the ultimate *usus loquendi* for the explication of any of its contents. Ernesti wanted to reserve this possibility, at least as a final means of adjudicating apparent contradictions and intractable obscurities in the text. But the fact that this possibility could not be sustained on the philological-historical grounds he allowed as the proper means of establishing usage led to its demise at the hands of his successors. They were quite right in regarding the canonical location of an element of tradition as irrelevant to a determination of its original meaning. And so long as the meaning of the text is to be determined exclusively in accord with the usage of its human producers, the canon can have no positive role in interpretation. As James Barr has observed, "No one redacted the Bible as a whole,"[29] so it is impossible to posit a human "authorship" to which the Bible as a single document might be assigned.

That fact is not fatal to the hermeneutical use of the canon, however, if such use is grounded instead—as was traditionally the case—in the decision to regard God, and not some particular human agent, as the "author" of scripture as a whole. Ernesti, of course, assumed as much, and was therefore confident of an ultimate coherence among the scriptural texts, since "God is not incapable of seeing what is consistent, and what is contradictory; nor can he forget, when he speaks, what was said on former occasions."[30] Although we cannot share his confidence that the various human authors of this material, individually considered, will not finally contradict each other—indeed, the evidence is to the contrary in a significant number of cases—we may nonetheless read scripture *as if it were* a whole, and as if the author of the whole were God. I say "as if," because my aim at present is not to offer a defense of such a reading, but only to suggest what the decision to read scripture this way implies.

Two major implications of this decision for our interpretation of a scriptural text seem apparent. The first regards what we take to be the scope of the utterance. Naively put, the decision prompts us to ask concerning the text, Why is God telling us this? What is the force of this utterance, construed as a component of God's self-disclosure to humankind? The second implication regards the context of the utterance: it is to be read in the light of the whole scriptural canon. These two implications are obviously closely related.

As to the first: Just as the umpire's "You're out!" differs from mine in that, among other things, it "makes" the runner out and allows the game to proceed accordingly, so "God was in Christ reconciling the world to himself" taken as God's own utterance differs from the same remark understood as issuing from, say, a given theologian. Coming from the theologian, the assertion might, for instance, be ventured as a hypothesis supported by any of various sorts of evidence. Coming from God, the utterance has a self-revelatory function. It is not an opinion, but a declaration. The substance of such a declaration might well be something which no one except God is in a position to communicate. Its primary aim may not be to resolve a Christological puzzle, but to transform the relationship between God and humankind. That is, as God's utterance the remark has a somewhat different force, and a different range of implications comes into view. Likewise, "In the beginning God created the heavens and the earth," heard as God's utterance, may be a radically different sort of remark from the same words uttered by someone scandalized by a geologist's account of the earth's likely origin. The scope of the utterance in the former case may not be explanatory at all; it may be to depict the relationship between God and world in such a way as to enable human beings to attend properly to God, world, and themselves. Regarding one's environment and oneself as "creation" and God as "Creator" involves considerably more (and conceivably quite other) than holding a theory as to the origin of things. These examples need not be elaborated further. Their common point is only that this change in the assignment of the "authorship" of many scriptural passages may greatly affect our understanding of their scope, and thus of their implications. (It also clearly affects the question of their truth conditions, as I have tried elsewhere to show.[31])

As to the second consequence of a decision to regard God as the author of scripture: It should be reiterated that the possibility of taking the scriptural canon as the context of interpretation does not involve the negation of other possibilities, including in particular the ordinary critical-historical procedure of interpreting a text in its sociohistorical context. We are, quite patently, doing two different things with the text, not trying to do the same thing by two different and incompatible methods, when we take it in canonical and in historical context. Each approach has its legitimacy and its theological usefulness.

There is, moreover, a crucial difference between the way in which the "canonical sense" of scripture was often sought in precritical exegesis and the way in which we are able to seek it ourselves. The difference does not, as some have supposed, render the results of precritical exegesis useless, but it does substantially affect the way in which we may appropriate those results as well as the way in which we may ourselves proceed with the task. Ernesti articulates the assumption of precritical exegesis in this regard when he asserts that there can be no real contradiction in scripture. Where contradiction was apparent and could not be attributed to copyists' errors, interpreters traditionally sought to remove it through a reinterpretation of one or both texts involved—a solution that often meant the violation of their own proper sense to a greater or lesser extent. Their practice was to show what the texts *must* mean, given the impossibility of final contradiction. Ernesti's own reluctance to appeal to a canonical adjudication of meaning except in cases of necessity indicates his awareness of the tension between such a strategy and the ordinary explication of a text in terms of authorial usage; but because he accepted a view of inspiration according to which God could see to it that nothing contradictory to the main tenor of scripture occurred in any of its parts, he felt justified in retaining the practice. That justification is no longer open to anyone basically acquainted with what the critical-historical study of the biblical texts discloses. There is simply no way to harmonize the sense of all the individual components of scripture, understood on their own terms.

What we may do, however, is to substitute discrimination for harmonization, and to affirm the positive role of judgment in attaining the canonical sense of a text. (The term "canonical significance" might seem preferable to "canonical sense"; but because what is sought is the proper *use* of the text in its canonical context, there is warrant for using the latter term. The canon establishes a new *usus loquendi,* so to speak, a new way of employing the material in question, just as the body that enacts my resolution supplies a new context for its subsequent understanding. At this juncture—though certainly not at others—the substitution of "significance" for "sense" may be ill-advised, since it masks the fact that a new usage is under way.) For example, where some earlier interpreters may have seen it as their task to determine what the author of James "must have meant" in the light of what some other portions of the New Testament clearly indicate, our task is to determine, in that same light—but *after* we have read James on its own terms—in what way and with what qualifications the message of James may be received. The ultimate outcome may not be too far different, though the routes diverge considerably. In both cases there is an appeal to a standard outside the particular passage or text itself, except that in the former case it is applied straightforwardly as a standard of interpretation, while in the latter it becomes explicitly a standard of judgment which is employed to determine the appropriate canonical use of the text. Thus it may be possible to acknowledge, for example, a canonical use or canonical sense of James 2:17 ("So faith by itself, if it has no works, is dead"), which is decidedly different from its sense in its own historical context. (Here the potential contrast between "canonical sense" and "canonical significance" becomes actual: James 2:17 may have a valid canonical *sense*, a proper use in canonical context, while its canonical *significance* on its own terms may be nil.) It is not accidental that the canonical appropriation of this theme in James generally takes it in the softer form represented by James 2:26. "Faith without works is dead" is not quite the affront to *sola fide* which the claim of the earlier verse in the same chapter presents. The form in which the text is canonically "remembered" indicates in part the qualifications with which the text is adapted for use.

Whichever way this reinterpretation of texts within the canonical context is achieved, it undoubtedly involves some loss of the sharp individuality of the diverse voices which might be heard in scripture: their sacrifice, it may be thought, to the cause of a unitary reading of scripture. It would be not only unfortunate but theologically indefensible if these voices were to be silenced—outshouted by God, so to speak—and their reality denied, particularly now that critical-historical study has increased our awareness of the humanity of these authors and thus of our commonality with them, and has enabled us to be both profoundly challenged by and thoroughly critical of what they have to say. This gives us all the more reason to insist upon the difference between our approach to the problem of seeking the coherence of scripture and the approach of our forebears, at the same time that we acknowledge a common aim: that of perceiving and following the plain sense of scripture as a whole as the Word of God. Some consideration of the character of that perceiving and following—the "inner side of explication," to adopt Schleiermacher's figure—is now in order before we turn to a more thorough examination of the hermeneutical significance of the canon.

Pursuing the traditional threefold distinction of *explicatio, meditatio,* and *applicatio* as the three dimensions or moments of scriptural interpretation, we will now consider *meditatio,* or "the transition of what is said into the thinking of the reader or hearer," as Barth described it.[32] This task is not separable from the task of explication either in aim or in execution, since on the one hand the accurate explication of the verbal sense of a text depends upon our own mastery of the concepts it involves, and on the other hand our mastery of those concepts is guided by the sense of the text which explication discloses. We are indeed concerned with two sides of a single exercise. *Meditatio* is not an introspective venture carried out at a remove from the text. If it is to be the reader's "realization" of the text, which enables the reader not only to understand the text (i.e., to fulfill the aim of *explicatio*) but also to understand *through* the text (i.e., to consider and embark upon *applicatio*), it must be controlled closely and constantly by the text.

When Jonathan Edwards inquires what scripture teaches concerning the end for which God created the world, he finds that the most adequate and comprehensive answer is: for God's own glory. But what, he then asks, is meant by "the glory of God"? At this point Edwards embarks upon a lengthy and careful examination of the principal instances in scripture where the glory of God is depicted or where the term itself and its functional equivalents otherwise find significant employment. At its conclusion, he offers no summary statement of findings, no drawing together of these threads. Instead, he remarks upon his procedure: "It is confessed that there is a degree of obscurity in these definitions; but perhaps an obscurity which is unavoidable, through the imperfection of language, and words being less fitted to express things of so sublime a nature. And therefore the thing may possibly be better understood, by using many words and a variety of expressions, by a particular consideration of it, as it were by parts, than by any short definition."[33] Ludwig Wittgenstein might well have applauded Edwards' practice in this instance, although with some demurrer as to the alleged imperfections of language which make the practice necessary. For Wittgenstein, this is simply how one teaches and learns the use of a concept: through the presentation and mastery of significant instances of its use. Examples have not only an illustrative purpose, ancillary to a straightforward explanation. They *are* the straightforward approach. As John Wisdom remarks, "Examples are the final food of thought."[34] They nourish thought and enable conceptual growth in a way that abstract discussion cannot, precisely because examples are embedded in the situations in which the pertinent conceptual abilities are to be exercised. Examples invite the learner to enter the situation, look around, and follow the action. They specify, at least by implication, the sorts of circumstances in which the concept comes into play: the conditions which evoke it or which it addresses, and the ways in which it is to be used under those conditions.

There are at least two reasons for the necessary recourse to examples in cases where one is attempting to teach or learn a genuinely new concept. The first is that concepts, objectively considered, are creatures of history: they come into being, are molded and occasionally transformed through their complex and flexible relationships to other concepts and to the particularities of human existence, and may even fade and wither. The lives of concepts are inextricably related to the lives of actual persons and communities.[35] Therefore the concept one learns is always shaped by contingent circumstances, and its mastery requires reference to those circumstances. (Think, for instance, of the ways in which concepts of "honor" and "shame" vary enormously from culture to culture, not only in their range of appropriate application—what is thought honorable or shameful—but in what each intrinsically involves.) Jonathan Edwards was no doubt aware that "glory" can mean many things and can conjure up widely differing associations. He could not rely upon some general acquaintance with the term to produce in his hearers a right understanding of the concept of the glory of God. That concept had to be imparted through the marshaling and invoking of what Edwards took to be normative examples of its use in scripture.

The second reason is the obverse of the first. Just as concepts are creatures of history whose configurations demand "a particular consideration," to use Edwards' phrase, so our acquisition and use of concepts is a historical process. It is within particular circumstances that one learns, say, regret or gratitude or hope, and the language that goes with them. Concepts relate to human capabilities, discovered, formed, and exercised within a life which is itself shaped by contingencies.

There is a close connection between the way we read those contingencies and the way we come to understand ourselves, in the double sense of self-knowledge set out in Chapter II, that is, knowledge that consists in our being enabled both to perceive and to enact who we are. Regret, for instance, does not just happen, *ex nihilo;* it arises upon a particular perception of one's situation. Circumstances make it appropriate or inappropriate, call it forth or give it no opportunity. But "circumstances" here means "circumstances as read." It is my own depiction of my situation—or the depiction that I adopt—which renders its components to me in their significance and which simultaneously nurtures the emotions, attitudes, and other capabilities with which I engage the situation. (This is not to deny that a particular feeling or predisposition may shape my depiction of my situation. The traffic undoubtedly moves in both directions. But it is the depiction, nevertheless, which enables me to name the feeling, to own the predisposition, to modify, to encourage, or even to dismiss it.) One does not learn concepts in the abstract, and store them up in expectation of eventual use. One learns concepts within the situations which call for them, in the exigencies of living. Examples, then, serve not only to depict the conventional uses of a concept but also to evoke in the learner a sense of the situation, the problem or the possibility to which the concept speaks. An example works to the extent that one is able to engage with it.

It is thus that, as W. B. Gallie observes, stories teach children feelings—and, we may add, a host of other sorts of concepts. Stories depict the conditions under which various human capacities may arise and develop, and show how those capacities change and are changed by the situation. The classic interweaving of "character and circumstance," with ample scope for the development of relevant detail, subthemes, and variations, ranks stories among the most effective sorts of "examples" by which concepts are conveyed. Of course, when a story sets out to be exemplary it is often less effective, because attention to realistic contingency has been sacrificed to the message. This discourages the reader's or hearer's imaginative participation in the story, since the story is too barren or too obviously contrived to be believable. There is a limit to the suspension of disbelief, however willing. To put the point in functional terms: the story must be followable. It must be possible to sense the fitness of the interplay of character and circumstance—even if what is fitting in a given instance can neither be predicted nor explained in any other way than by going over the story again, calling attention to its particular features.[36] (The inexplicability of "fitness" in nonnarrative terms is itself a sort of evidence for the irreplaceability of examples in conceptual training.)

Of course, there are times when the reader fails to follow the story, to grasp the fit, or to see the point of the example, not because of any defect in the depiction itself, but because of a deficiency in the reader. Sometimes a willing suspension of disbelief is not enough; or to put it in terms with more theological resonance, sometimes suspending disbelief takes more than a willingness to entertain a novel perspective. Whatever may be the case with other sorts of examples, this is certainly true of the task of conceptual growth pertinent to Christian understanding. *Meditatio* may be a quite active and strenuous discipline, namely, the discipline of endeavoring, by God's grace, to let the concepts found in the Christian texts take root in one's life. To give them room, weeds must be cleared, soil prepared, nourishment found. The possibilities that the texts present must not only be entertained in imagination but tried out in practice. In fact, whether they may be rightly entertained in imagination at all prior to their being imparted through practice is open to serious doubt. Calvin's dictum, "All right knowledge of God is born of obedience," may be taken as a reminder of the connection between understanding and practice.[37]

But the connection between *explicatio* and *meditatio*, between following the verbal sense of a text and achieving its conceptual concomitance, should be evident: The first line of approach, in acquiring or testing our understanding of either, is to study the *usus loquendi*, primarily through examples. Such was the approach advocated by Ernesti, and followed in practice by Jonathan Edwards in the illustration just considered. Ernesti recommended the continuous and frequent reading of the pertinent exemplary passages, to fix them in mind and to gain a sense of the range of the usage in question. The examples serve to teach the grammar of the concept under study, in an inclusive sense of "grammar";

that is, they show not only the place and function of the concept in the language but its place and function in human life.

But examples can do so only insofar as the interpreter or learner is able to infer from them what the concept in question amounts to, by virtue of a competence already possessed (as, e.g., when I can gather from the usage of the German *schwarz* that it is basically equivalent to "black"), or when an example can itself function as a teacher. An example can teach, for instance, by informing the interpreter of the conditions under which one might learn the concept in question, or in some cases by actually inducing those conditions, as a parable or a dramatic narrative can. Here the example assumes the role of one who trains a person in the use of a concept. But even when such help is not forthcoming from the text or from the examples that can be adduced, or when it is not sufficient, interpretation may not leave these behind to go in quest of understanding elsewhere. Rather, what is needed is training in the use of the concepts involved, of the sort which another human being who already has the concepts may provide; and this training will itself involve concrete examples. Ordinarily, of course, we are trained in these competencies by other living human beings and do not rely wholly upon texts for our nurture. One function of the church is to serve as the community that assists and sustains persons in their growth in Christian understanding. But that community is the church only so long as it is bound to scripture as the text from which it initially receives that understanding, and by which its understanding is constantly tested. How that testing is to be envisioned and realized—that is, how scripture functions normatively in the formation of Christian understanding—is the next question to be faced.

It is beyond the scope of this inquiry, and, I think, beyond the scope of hermeneutics properly understood, to provide an account of how understanding "happens," whether in an epistemological or in a psychological framework. Intriguing and important as is, say, that crucial transition from rote learning to comprehension, or that distinction which Gilbert Ryle drew between "drill" and "training"—"Drill dispenses with intelligence, training develops it"[38]—it does not belong to this inquiry to do more than to observe them and to insist on their importance. The criteria for understanding with which we are concerned, and indeed the criteria that generally govern the use of the term, have to do with demonstrable capabilities and not with "inner processes" however conceived and described, as Wittgenstein was at some pains to point out. It does pertain to hermeneutics to reflect upon these criteria (in our case, with regard to the aims of Christian understanding) and upon the conditions under which those criteria have some hope of being satisfied.

The Christian understanding of scripture is primarily instrumental to the knowledge of God. That is, it aims to be not only an understanding *of* scripture but an understanding *through* scripture as well. The preceding conjoint treatment of the tasks of verbal explication and conceptual mastery was governed by that fact. But there is a third factor to be considered. In addition to *explicatio* and *meditatio*, theological hermeneutics must treat of *applicatio*, or, as Barth says, of the transition from the *sensus* to the *usus scripturae*.[39] Scripture can obviously be used in many ways. How should it be used? What are the Christian uses of the text once it has been grasped? This critical question also belongs to theological hermeneutics, in that scripture itself is held to provide the answer. That is, the Bible is affirmed to be the canon of Christian understanding: not simply its source or its record, but its judge. The proper understanding and use of the scriptural canon is thus a major hermeneutical topic.

IV
The Canon
of
Christian Understanding

At the close of the first chapter, I suggested that Christian theology, as a critical inquiry into the truthfulness of Christian witness, asks two questions concerning any given instance of such witness: Is it truly Christian? Is it true? Neither question, of course, belongs to theology alone. The first might be raised by, for example, a historian of religions seeking by some means to distinguish the Christian from the non-Christian in the data that are under study. Similar questions could be raised as to the "truly Buddhist," "truly Muslim," and so forth. The second question, as to the truth of Christian witness, might be asked by a philosopher wishing to describe and perhaps to adjudicate the truth claims involved in the Christian message, or in some particular version or sample of it. Christian theology does not raise unique questions about its subject matter. It characteristically pursues these two questions, in conjunction, because they are the primary questions which any responsible representation of the Christian witness must be prepared to answer concerning itself.

There is a hermeneutical component to each of these two lines of inquiry, since before one can judge either the Christianness or the truth of a statement—before one can even clearly determine just what procedures for judgment are in order—one needs to understand what one is judging. The hermeneutical task thus precedes and accompanies the critical task: accompanies as well as precedes because within the process of critical reflection launched by these questions the need may arise for a further clarification or fuller explication of the data in ways that cannot always be anticipated. However, theological hermeneutics has a particular responsibility toward the first of these questions, that is, as to the Christianness of putative Christian witness. It has this responsibility because the criterion by which this question is to be answered—the *canon*, or "rule," of Christian witness —is itself an object of interpretative inquiry. According to the Christian witness itself, its Christianness or "Christian aptness" (to borrow David Kelsey's phrase[40]) is to be tested by the canon of scripture; and the question which that affirmation immediately raises is: How is that to be done? How is the canon of scripture to be brought to bear upon a particular instance or situation of Christian witness? It is ordinarily conceded that an utterance or action is not "in accord with scripture" in this sense simply by virtue of having an apparent precedent, even a verbatim verbal precedent, in the Bible. Christian witness can be "scriptural" or "biblical" without replicating words and phrases in the Bible, just as one's words and actions can be "unscriptural" or "unbiblical" even if one is quoting scripture in the process. How is scripture to be understood and used in its canonical function? This is a major question for theological hermeneutics.

There is, of course, a further question to be raised about the canon, namely, the question as to the propriety of the church's (or of a church's) identification of the criterion of Christian witness. Should the Bible be affirmed as the canon? If so, in which of its forms (e.g., with or without "apocrypha")? If not, what revision or relocation of the

canon should be accepted? The full pursuit of such questions transcends and integrates several disciplines of theological inquiry.[41] The present investigation of the canon,
however, will be much more restricted. It will be directed
by the hermeneutical question as to how the present canon
of scripture might be understood in its canonical function
—not because the wider issues of scriptural authority and
canonicity are foreclosed, but because this is one proper
service of theological hermeneutics to that wider discussion, as well as its normal responsibility as a theological
discipline. Accepting the biblical canon as "given," and
bracketing the broader range of questions concerning theological and churchly authority, how is Christian understanding to be governed by this canon?

The situation in which this question is to be treated is
complicated by the fact that the Bible has a variety of functions within Christian life and witness. To mention a few
of its roles: It is our principal means of access to the communities of faith whose product it is; our primary, and
occasionally our only, source of data—such as it is—concerning various historical figures, including Jesus; a collection of texts for meditation; the source of innumerable images and metaphors, ideas and modes of expression which
have found incorporation into the church's thought,
speech, and life. Scripture is, in short, the primary source
for Christian witness: the main, though certainly not the
only, source of the data, the concepts, and the language out
of which Christian witness is formed and nourished.

However, to acknowledge this source function of scripture is not yet to come to terms with its *canonical* function.
To put it briefly, not every use of scripture is "scriptural,"
while not everything that is "scriptural" derives from scripture. "Scriptural" in this usage refers to the canonical function of scripture, as distinct from its function as source. The
material we regard as canonical Christian scripture has or-

dinarily served simultaneously these two major, logically distinct, functions. Yet the distinction has generally gone unobserved. That is, although scripture has served this dual purpose, the duality has seldom come in for reflective consideration, and its implications remain to be fully explored. The neglect of the distinction is due in part to the close interrelatedness and mutual reinforcement of these functions in the church's traditional practice, and in part to the fact that the possibility of a critical examination of the sources of the Christian tradition, including scripture, is a relatively recent development, so that methodological self-consciousness about the uses of scripture in these two ways has been late in arising and is still far from secure. An awareness of the distinction and what it involves is vital, however, because in its absence, one of these two functions will continually tend to assimilate or to obscure the other, so that the church is denied ready access to both. The results may range from the uncritical enforcement of random scriptural texts as normative, to the serious erosion of any clear idea as to how scripture might function to authorize Christian witness at all.

When interpreters become preoccupied with the canonical status and function of biblical texts, the historical character of these same texts—their context in and continuity with the history of tradition—is quite likely to be ignored, downplayed, or even denied. Such was the case during the period of Protestant orthodoxy, when it was thought (not without some justification under the circumstances) that the defense of the "scripture principle" necessitated the denial that scripture could be properly approached also as tradition. It took a deliberate and resolute *apologia* for the propriety of a free historical investigation of scripture, coupled with inescapable evidence of its possibility and its fruitfulness, to break the hold of orthodoxy and give the church renewed access to scripture as source. Unfortunately, that *apologia* was often perceived by both sides as entailing an attack upon the canonical function of scripture as such, and not simply upon the ways in which the envisioning and defending of that function had led to untenable claims about scripture on the part of orthodox dogmaticians.[42] In any case, as the investigation of scripture along the lines appropriate to its character as primary source material became well established, questions arose with increasing intensity as to just how and why this material, with all its internal diversity, historical contingency, obvious similarities to other ancient material, and so forth, is supposed to have some sort of coherent normative bearing upon the contemporary life and witness of the Christian community, especially now that the community is burdened with all this historical knowledge of its own canon. In this situation, which is still largely our own, some clarification of the distinctive logic of the canonical use of scripture is an urgent necessity, both to preserve the integrity of that use and to prevent any rejection or subversion of the ongoing critical study of scripture as source.

In what follows, I want first to characterize each of these functions in sufficient detail to make their distinctiveness apparent, and then to move beyond the formal distinction to propose a way of construing scripture as canon which may help us to see how scripture-as-canon may be brought to bear upon the Christian interpretation and use of scripture generally, that is, upon the question of *applicatio.*

"Scripture" and "canon" are not synonymous terms, although they are often applied to the same body of texts and are used interchangeably when their distinction is not at issue.[43] A canon is a standard of judgment; the term is functionally equivalent to "criterion" or to "rule" in many respects. A canon need not take the form of a collection of scripture. It might be, for example, a formula, a creed, or even an unwritten consensus. Nor, for that matter, does the designation of a text or texts as "scripture" necessarily bestow a strictly canonical status and function, as the phenomenon of extracanonical scripture shows. The emergence of the scriptural canon in the early church was not due to any *a priori* necessity for the identification of "canon" with "scripture," but is rather a development worth pondering along with its alternatives: What, if anything, makes a canon of *scripture* particularly apt in the case of the Christian community? This question will come in for some consideration below. At the moment, the point to note is that the selection and arrangement of a portion of the community's scripture to constitute its canon is a decisive development. Among its interesting consequences is the fact that this portion of scripture henceforth was to do double duty: serving both as scripture—that is, as part of the primary written tradition, the source material upon which the community draws in its continuing reflection upon its life and witness—and as the canon by which that life and witness are to be assessed and corrected. The "norming" function of canonical scripture does not replace its "traditioning" function, nor does it simply include it. Thus any adequate interpretative approach to this body of texts must allow for the realization and the interplay of both.

In its role as source, scripture is the repository of the formative traditions of the community. It does not encompass the totality of those traditions, nor does it necessarily include all the important elements (however such importance is to be determined) of the traditions from which it springs. But it contains those elements of early tradition which the community has perceived as decisive for its own identity and purpose, and has thus preserved. As the community's memory, it is a major resource for its present thinking, yielding a rich supply of images and ideas, theological insights, stylistic patterns, conceptual developments

and distinctions, historical data and interpretation, to provoke the community to thought and to equip it for its thinking and speaking. The discovery and exhibition of the varied contents of this resource by every means available is a
continuing task, essential to the health of the community.

Since the rise of historical criticism, the pursuit of this
task is not confined to the study of the texts as they stand.
They can be interrogated further, as earlier layers of tradition are discernible beneath the canonical form of the texts.
It is possible to reconstruct the history of traditions which
led to the formation of the canonical documents, so that
more and more of the life and thought of the early community and its antecedents becomes available to inform present reflection. At the same time, the study of the historical
setting of these texts and their component traditions permits a fuller understanding of all this material, a clearer
view of the issues and situations being addressed, of the
force of the affirmations and denials being made, and of the
forms of thought and expression involved. There can be no
doubt that our present knowledge of primitive Christianity
and of the history of Israel has been enormously enriched
through such critical-historical study, that is, through the
practice of those disciplines by which a text or a tradition
is broken out of its canonical context and restored to the
context of its historical development, its *Sitz im Leben*,
where it may take on quite a different sense. The early
"precanonical" communities recover their voice, and we
gain some understanding of their situations and their concerns. And this means that the potential of scripture as
source—not only as historical source material but as resource for reflection upon the possibilities and responsibili-
ties of Christian witness—has been considerably enhanced
by the development of these disciplines of study.

Of course, the relevant source material for these inquiries
cannot be restricted in principle to the canonical texts and

their earlier forms and ingredients. Extracanonical material not only may be useful, it may be strictly necessary to an accurate elucidation of the sense of various elements of the canonical material itself. A study of the extracanonical as well as the canonical Christian literature of the New Testament period provides a much more comprehensive view of the actual character and historical fortunes of early Christianity than a study that restricts itself to the New Testament literature, and has a bearing on one's assessment of the significance of the growth of the New Testament as well. As historical source, the canonical material is entitled to no privileged position which cannot be sustained on the basis of critical-historical study; its reliability—for example, over against rival accounts of early Christian developments—cannot be presumed, but must be examined. In its role as source, canonical scripture is useful insofar as it allows us access to a considerable portion of early tradition. But to treat this material as a unity, and in isolation from its historical surroundings, would be to impose serious limitations upon our potential understanding of what this source offers to us precisely as source.

It should be obvious from what has been said that scripture in its canonical function cannot norm the understanding of scripture as source. The latter sort of investigation has its own proper procedures, derived in the main from the disciplines of historical inquiry and from the hermeneutical reflection proper to such inquiry. The aims of this investigation require that it be free from any attempt to weight the results in favor of a canonically derived interpretation. It is important to note that the legitimacy of a canonical use of scripture is not in question here; what is questionable is a confusion of the aims and procedures proper to these two distinct uses of the textual material, since such a confusion can only thwart the realization of either. It is not the aim of the study of scripture as source either to vindicate or to supplant the use of scripture as canon, any more than it is the role of scripture as canon to direct or to challenge its study as source.

To designate a body of scripture as the canon is not merely to draw boundaries around that portion of scripture to indicate its particular importance or its more or less official acceptance as scripture, though that view of the significance of the designation is not uncommon. The canonization of Christian scripture is more adequately understood as the bestowal upon these texts of a specific function, rather than simply as their churchly recognition or their exaltation to a higher status. This is not a claim as to what was intended or anticipated by those responsible, in whatever way, for the development of the Christian canon or for the eventual application of that term to the collection. It is a claim as to how the subsequent functioning of these writings in the community may best be understood. James Barr, for one, is skeptical of any suggestion that we should attribute hermeneutical motives to the shapers of the canon. He regards the canon as "a delimitation of the margins of sacred scripture," not necessarily intended to serve as a context for interpretation or as an "exegetical principle" of some sort.[44] But whatever the intent, the establishment or recognition of the canon clearly has hermeneutical consequences.

To delimit the margins one way and not another inevitably defines a context for interpretation: If A and B are to be accepted as authoritative utterances, you read them in the light of each other; and you are less concerned to assure that your interpretation of either is consistent with C and D, which, even if part of the original context of A or B, do not have canonical status. Whether you proceed "precritically," that is, by considering what A and B "must mean" given their canonical juxtaposition, or "postcritically," by considering how the texts may now be taken and used given their common canonicity, you find that the drawing of margins around these texts establishes new relationships among them, and between them and extracanonical Christian tradition, past, contemporary, and future. That is to say, these texts together in this form are henceforth understood and used as a criterion of Christian witness, as a standard by which the "traditioning" activity of the Christian community is to be critically assessed and directed.

If the canonical force of these texts is to be realized, they must be approached in a somewhat different way than is proper to their study as sources of Christian tradition. First, they must be taken together, rather than taken apart. While a source study involves the provisional dismantling of the canon, the separation of texts from their canonical context and the distinguishing and re-relating of various elements within the texts themselves, a canonical reading of the texts requires that their relationship to one another be taken into account. The Bible is a singular canon, not a collection of individual canons; to acknowledge a text as canonical is to say that it *belongs to* the canon, not that it is *another* canon. So, rather than concentrating on each separate text as somehow authoritative in isolation from the rest, our prior task would seem to be to come to terms with the canon as a unity, and to see how its various parts may bear upon one another. A canonical reading will distinguish, but not separate, Old Testament from New, Torah from prophets, gospel from apostle. Nor will the pertinent relationships be restricted to cases of historical or literary dependence (i.e., canonically, one reads the Old Testament in the light of the New, as well as vice versa). How the unity of the canon is to be construed is, of course, a major question to be confronted in any canonical reading, as will be indicated more fully below. The way that question is answered largely determines the ways in which the texts may be "taken together."

A canonical reading will, naturally enough, have a primary interest in the texts in their "final" or canonical redaction. The prehistory of the individual documents is of less immediate relevance, except insofar as some later editorial work may have been contemporary with and even directly incidental to the process of canon formation in the early church. The church which acknowledged these texts as constitutive of its canon was largely unaware of their prehistory, at least in the sense in which that prehistory is accessible to modern critical study, even though there was some lively interest in questions of provenance and authenticity. It is, for example, the book of Exodus or the Gospel of Matthew which is canonically decisive, and not the various strands, strata, and sources of tradition which may lie behind either and which might be reconstructed as oral or written "works" in their own right. This does not mean that historical considerations are irrelevant to a canonical reading of the texts. Historical awareness of the ways in which a given writing was perceived and read at the time of the formation of the Christian canon may provide crucial insight into its canonical significance, while the history of its subsequent interpretation may well be relevant to one's own attempts at canonical exegesis.

Finally, a canonical reading of these texts will have some regard for the way they are ordered and grouped within the canon. It is significant, for example, that the early church did not simply add further writings to the Bible it inherited, but rather moved toward the distinction between two "testaments." Other features of the arrangement of the canonical writings may not be wholly accidental or trivial, and deserve some close consideration in the course of an inquiry into the unity and overall character of the canon, not because the received arrangement is "authoritative" (it may indeed prove to be in some respects fortuitous, arbitrary, or supported by assumptions and arguments which are no longer convincing), but because it can stimulate reflection upon possible construals of the canon as a unity.

What has been said here about the importance of the interrelatedness, the final forms, and the arrangement of the biblical texts from the standpoint of an interpreter interested in their canonical use, would be misunderstood if it were taken as an invitation to dismiss or to disregard the results of critical-historical investigation of the canonical material. Such investigation reveals the great diversity and sometimes conflicting tendencies represented in the material collected into the canon; it shows how early material has been sundered, recombined, rewritten, and transformed in the process which produced the "final" texts; and it leaves us with an inescapable sense of the historical contingency of the shaping of the canon as a whole. These findings do, in fact, seriously call into question some ways of justifying and of construing the scriptural canon, but they do not devastate the enterprise of canonical interpretation as such so long as its own distinctive assumptions and aims are observed. They tend rather to strengthen it in this respect, by showing that the use of scripture as canon is quite a different sort of thing from its use as a source of early Christian tradition and historical data.

A canon is a canon only in use; and it must be construed in a certain way before it can be used. If someone were to hand me a chunk of metal and identify it as a "standard," I might not know immediately what sort of standard it was to be—whether a standard of length, weight, color, hardness, value, metallic purity, conductivity, or of something still more exotic. I would need to know the sort of activity in which this object figures as a standard, and how it is to be regarded and used, before the statement that it is a standard will be very informative. Similarly, the bare statement that the Bible is the canon needs some elucidation before one knows how it is to be taken and used as canon: how it is to be put to work, under what circumstances, for what purposes. A number of possibilities, more or less remote, may easily be entertained in connection with the Bible's canonicity. Is it to be taken as a definitive assemblage of (sometimes cleverly disguised) doctrinal propositions? As a collection of instructive accounts of human behavior? As an anthology of exemplary sermons? As the true history of the world? For an imaginative interpreter coming fresh to this material, the great range of plausible construals may have an immobilizing impact. To another interpreter, of a different background and cast of mind, it may be obvious that there is only one possible way to characterize the canon, come what may. Either example suggests the importance of giving some attention to the process of construal, so that a deliberate and reasoned judgment—rather than either a forced or an arbitrary choice—may be made.

At least three considerations would appear relevant to the search for principles to guide a characterization of scripture in its canonical function. These are the form and content of the canon itself; the history of its use as canon; and the typical ways in which its role as canon is justified.

If the chunk of metal I am handed is spherical in shape, with no apparent markings on its surface, I would probably not be inclined to entertain the notion that it might be a standard of length. I might even regard with skepticism my informant's insistence that the object is indeed a standard of length, particularly if the informant's demonstrations of its functioning in that capacity seemed (as well they might) somewhat strained and contrived. I would want to know why this object was being put to this use, when they seem so unsuited to each other. In just the same way, the form and content of the biblical canon has *prima facie* relevance to a determination of its proper construal. If it is being forced into a use for which it seems particularly unsuited, or if some apparently important and pertinent features of the material are being disregarded, it is reasonable to expect some explanation. Of course, a cogent explanation might be furnished, but there is a clear burden of proof upon anyone who would offer a characterization of the canon which appears to violate the character of the canonical material itself. A depiction of the canon as essentially a historical record, or as a textbook of doctrine, would obviously encounter this sort of difficulty. On the other hand, of course, the fact that a particular construal seems to fit the material as we understand it is not by itself a decisive argument in its favor, since the same material may, in fact, be patient of several different uses. Just as one may not always correctly infer literary genre from literary structure, so the form and content of the canon do not necessarily define its use.

Use is indeed the major consideration. How does the canon actually come into play? In what activities has it a role, and how is it brought to bear upon those activities? The history of the use of the canon in the community is probably the most significant indication of the range, and of the relative value, of relevant possible construals. Of course, that use has been far from uniform or consistent throughout history. Both the relative importance of the canon in the ongoing life and thought of the community, and the specific ways in which it has been brought into play, have varied a great deal, so it is not possible to identify a paradigmatic construal and use on the basis of some historical or ecumenical consensus. It is, however, possible to distinguish various models or patterns of canonical use, and to ask relevant questions of each—for example, as to its effectiveness in actually enabling the canon to function as canon, and as to the sorts of problems incident upon its use. A pattern of construal with some demonstrated effectiveness in a variety of situations, and with the power to withstand (if not to resolve) the problems created by its own adoption, would have some obvious immediate advantage over a proposal that has no historical precedent or near relative.

The third consideration has to do with the sorts of justification offered for the role of the canon in the community. Why is the canon the canon? Before addressing this question, we will do well to ponder the sort of question it is. In what sense may a canon be justified?

Again, an analogy may help. If someone points to a length of metal on display, and says to me, "That's the standard meter," I may ask, "Why is that the standard meter?" There are several ways that question could be answered. My informant could respond: "Because it's exactly one meter long. Here's a tape measure—see for yourself!" Or I could be given a brief history of the standardization of measurements, indicating the developments leading to the establishment of this particular standard. Or, the answer could be, "Because whatever corresponds to this is one meter long." The first answer represents a misguided attempt to justify the standard by demonstrating its conformity to the very thing it is supposed to norm. The second shows how the standard came to be recognized as such, that is, why this particular thing came to be given this role. The third answer indicates most clearly and directly what *makes* this the standard—why it is right to call this the standard meter.

The same three sorts of response could be offered to the query, "Why is the canon the canon?" Answers of the first sort (e.g., "Because it is marvelously consonant with Jesus' own teaching," "Because its content, properly interpreted, corresponds perfectly with the church's dogma") would undercut the very claim they are supposed to justify, by appealing in effect to another standard and thereby showing that the "canon" is *not* the canon. The other two sorts of response are proper and helpful: the second, an account of how these writings came to be accepted as the canon, shows what sort of authorization this canon is taken to have; while the third sort of reply simply states what makes the canon the canon. ("Why is this the canon of Christian witness?" "Because what is in accord with this is what we call Christian witness.")

Now, it is clear that the canon cannot be "justified" in the first of these ways. To attempt this sort of justification is to show that one has misunderstood the concept and function of canon. What the third sort of response offers is not strictly a justification at all, but rather the kind of reminder about the concept and function of canon which is needed to prevent the first sort of attempt at justification. It clarifies the use of the term "canon." It is the second of these approaches to justification which may be most pertinent to the task of finding an adequate characterization of the scriptural canon. The process through which these texts became recognized as the canon of Christian witness may be studied with an eye toward the discovery of the particular pattern of authorization involved here. That is, it may disclose how this particular set of texts assumed the key role it has in the ordering of the community's thought and life, and how this canon derives, holds, and exercises its authority. In such an inquiry into the authorization of the canon, it is important to guard against any tendency to assume that the authority of scripture as canon must be of the same kind as the authority of these texts as primary sources of tradition. In the latter role, the texts are "authoritative" in the same sense that the historian's primary sources are—that is, insofar as they are the basic and indispensable means of access to that of which they speak. The authorization of the *canon*, however, may take quite another route. That possibility must at least be kept open.

As we pursue this inquiry, the distinction between the way the canon assumed its role and the way that role was explicitly understood and justified at the time is also impor-

tant. It is entirely possible that the early church and its
leading thinkers may not have clearly understood *why* the
canon is the canon, even while they were engaged in acknowledging (and arguing) *that* it is. To some extent, they
may have been in the position of having to offer explana-
tions for a *fait accompli*, or a *fait-accompli*-in-the-making.
This is not to suggest that the canon in its fullness simply
"imposed itself" upon the church to universal acclaim while
the deliberations of bishops and theologians had negligible
impact on the process. Such a reading of events cannot be
historically sustained. There were lingering questions as to
the canonicity of certain books not only in the minds of
scholars, but in and among the Christian communities, and
historians might point to particular cases in which the in-
tervention of one thinker or the momentary ascendancy of
one party gave the edge to one book or sealed the fate of
another.[45] And we may have to acknowledge that in some
instances those responsible for these developments may
have been mistaken not only in their judgments (even
though some mistaken judgments, such as judgments about
authorship, may have turned out for the better), but also in
thinking that these judgments were the relevant ones.
Again, judgments that are pertinent to a determination of
the reliability of a text as a source of tradition may not be
pertinent to the question of its fitness for a place in the
canon. The fact that such distinctions were, in all likeli-
hood, absent from the minds of leading figures in the discussions of what should constitute canonical Christian scripture, suggests that caution should be used in appropriating
their arguments and findings.

Whether or not we are distressed by the sheer contingency of the process of canon formation, by the ambiguity
at the margins of the canon, by the possibility that we might
be unable to offer any clear reasons why, for example, Jude
should be in the New Testament and I Clement outside, all

depends on our total understanding of the canon and its function. If the value and validity of the canon rest upon the clear distinctiveness of its content from everything outside (as has sometimes been assumed), then the canon is in serious difficulty. If the effectiveness of the canon is diminished by the presence of ambiguity or vagueness around its margins or even within, the critical-historical investigation of the canon-forming process, no less than of its content, may yield intolerable results. But these are open questions, which should not be resolved before an attempt is made to understand how the canon works, how this material is actually to be taken and used in its canonical function. Apparent problems may turn out to be less serious than was assumed. Even vagueness and ambiguity are not always defects. It is not mere hyperbole, but a provocative theological remark when W. G. Kümmel takes the uncertainty about the bounds of the canon as a reminder that "the Word became flesh."[46]

In order for this discussion to be carried farther, it will be necessary to develop a brief construal of the canon, which will indicate one way in which the canon as a whole may be conceived and brought into play. Clearly many different construals of the canon are possible. Each one, however promising, gives rise to its own set of questions and problems, some fairly obvious, others latent. It may be only after some experience with the use of the canon thus construed that one is in a position to assess the values and limitations of a construal and to suggest revisions or alternatives.

This construal takes its initial cue from the fact that one of the most common and consistent ways in which Christians from the earliest times onward have perceived their own witness has been as a participation in God's own self-communication. The community, formed and informed by God's Spirit, has spoken God's Word.[47] Though the "Word of God" strictly transcends any particular occasion of human utterance, New Testament writers variously applied the term to "Old Testament" material, to the teachings of Jesus, and by extension to the Christian kerygma itself. The texts which evolved from that kerygma came gradually and naturally—though not without ambiguity and risk—to share that designation. It was from this material, in which the community had heard the Word of God and from which it expected to hear that word again, that the canon was formed. The canon, then, functions to show what the Word of God is. This is not to say that the words of the text may be simply identified as "God's words." But when the canon, as such, is properly activated, it norms all other Christian witness—that is, it enables a judgment as to whether or how some other human utterance may also participate in God's self-disclosive word.

But how does the canon exercise this norming function? The form of the canon itself may indicate something of its mode of functioning. When one regards the biblical canon as a whole, the centrality to it of a narrative element is difficult to overlook: not only the chronological sweep of the whole, from creation to new creation, including the various events and developments of what has sometimes been called "salvation history," but also the way the large narrative portions interweave and provide a context for the remaining materials so that they, too, have a place in the ongoing story, while these other materials—parables, hymns, prayers, summaries, theological expositions—serve in different ways to enable readers to get hold of the story and to live their way into it. This overall narrative character of the canon, together with its designation as Word of God, suggests that the canon might plausibly be construed as a story which has God as its "author." It is a story in which real events and persons are depicted in a way that discloses their relationship to God and to God's purposes; a story that finally involves and relates all persons and events, and which, as it is told and heard in the power of God's Spirit, becomes the vehicle of God's own definitive self-disclosure. God is not only the author of this story but its chief character as well; so that as the story unfolds we come to understand who God is. And because God is not only the chief character but also the author, the story's disclosure is God's self-disclosure. We become acquainted with God as the one who is behind this story and within it.[48]

The canon, thus construed, norms Christian witness not by providing sample statements by which to test other statements, nor by providing ideals of some other sort, but by reminding the community of the identity of the one whose word they bear. The canon may not contain, explicitly or *in nuce*, every statement the church may want or need to make in its witness. But the church may and must ask, concerning those words which it is moved to receive or to utter in God's name and concerning those actions which it hopes to interpret or to perform, whether they are indeed consistent with the identity of the God whom the canonical story discloses. That which is "scriptural" or "biblical," in the sense of "authorized by the scriptural canon," is that which does accord with that identity.

Put in a somewhat different way, yet using the same basic construal, the canon is the story through which Jesus Christ is made present anew to the community. This way of expressing the point of the construal enables us to see its relationship to a classical Reformation understanding of biblical authority. Using Robert Clyde Johnson's helpful distinction between the often-equated terms "norm" and "criterion," we may say that the biblical canon is the *criterion* of Christian witness, the "functional critical instrument" by which the Christianness of the church's witness is to be assessed; but this criterion derives its authority from the true *norm* of Christian witness, Jesus Christ, the absolute and underivative "author" of God's self-disclosure.[49] The criterion (i.e., the canon) functions properly to authorize witness only when it enables access to the norm by which it is itself authorized and empowered (i.e., Jesus Christ). The criterion may not replace the norm, but can only re-present it. Scripture is only properly activated as canon when its activation allows an apprehension of the one who is both its author and its subject. So, counter to Protestant orthodoxy's tendency to exalt scripture to the status of absolute norm, we must say that it is Jesus Christ, not scripture, who is *norma normans sed non normata*. This does not in the least compromise the authority of scripture. It only reinforces the grammatical point that "authority" is a functional term. Authority is always ultimately derived from and exercised in obedience to an "authorizer" which is not itself an authority, but rather a *source* of authority. In this sense, the authority of scripture can be properly and fully acknowledged only when it is understood that scripture is not to be confused with that norm which it is authorized to disclose.[50]

Earlier in this chapter the question was posed: What makes a canon of *scripture* particularly apt, given the range of other possible canonical forms? We may restate the question somewhat more precisely now: What makes this quasi-narrative collection, this story with supporting material, particularly useful as a canon of Christian understanding? Why not condense it, or at least streamline it, so as to clarify the heart of the Christian message and eliminate some confusion and ambiguity? Without launching a full theological discussion of the possibility and desirability of modifying the canon, we may mention some considerations bearing on the aptness of this canon. Of course, these considerations do not "explain" why we happen to have the canon we do, nor do they defend just this canon against all other options. They only suggest why the character of this canon apparently enables it to serve its purpose.

It would appear that a short formula (say, "Jesus is Lord") would have some immediate advantages over the cumbersomeness of the scriptural canon. It is highly "portable," that is, easily assimilable to many contexts, readily identifiable and apparently understandable. But these are also its fatal liabilities, so far as its canonical usefulness is concerned. The confession, "Jesus is Lord," only makes sense within a story. Its value as a confession or reminder of Christian witness depends upon its users' and hearers' acquaintance with some account of who Jesus is and what it means (or how it happens) that he is Lord. A hearer who lacks this context can always make one up, or ask for one to be supplied—but what is there to assure that the account imagined or offered is Christianly appropriate? "Jesus is Lord," or a similar short formula, is simply not enough to go on. Because it can move quite easily from story home to story home, it can mean a great many, not always compatible, things. Its users might have nothing in common except the words, unless they have been given a common context. But if the context itself has no normative force, there is no control in principle over the interpretation and use of the formula. To cite James Sanders' two desiderata for a canon, the formula has high adaptability but no stability.[51] The *words* are stable, but apart from some larger context ruling their use, they can provide no stable criterion, only at best the illusion of one. Only in its scriptural matrix does "Jesus is Lord" convey the associations which enable it to function as Christian confession. Similarly, even a longer symbol such as the Apostles' Creed serves best to remind its users of the biblical canon. It abstracts and interprets certain features of the canonical narrative to guide the reflection and affirmation of the community of faith, but it does not replace that narrative. Its abstractions must be grounded in the particularity of scripture, from which they take their life.

Scripture provides the context for the interpretation and assessment of such formulas, and thus serves to define Christian understanding and to govern Christian witness, through offering, at the same time, both a coherent story from which terms like "Jesus" and "Lord" derive their sense, and innumerable supplementary examples, illustrations, reminders, and exercises to encourage our understanding participation in the narrative and to inculcate and strengthen those capacities which permit, in conjunction with the narrative, a right apprehension of God, world, and self. It is essential that the canon include within itself the means for this pedagogy; otherwise we would need a canon for the proper understanding of the canon, or some "authorized" interpretation which would, in effect, supplement or supplant the canon. But the price of this pedagogical richness is a canon full of homely stories, rough analogies, notes on sundry points, incomplete illustrations, verbal tricks, and so on—an unruly lot of heuristic devices, in and alongside the ongoing depiction of God's ways with the world. To grasp the fact that all this untidiness is *functional*, in ways in which a neat, compact, simple canon could not be, is to have broken the spell of that false idealization of the canon which is one of the greatest hindrances to its effective use in theology and church. The hermeneutical equivalent of the docetic heresy is the refusal to accept the humanity of the text, with all that it involves. Until that is accepted, as the very means of our participation in the knowledge of God, the canonical function of scripture will evade us.

The particularity of scripture, and its diversity—its ability to provide a multitude of concrete instances and examples, of varying kinds, to initiate its users into a conceptual skill, to permit some disclosure or insight, to enable the growth or correction of previous understanding—are thus major assets, when they are recognized as such. That they are also the occasion of serious conflict is undeniable. There is justification for Ernst Käsemann's oft-quoted claim that the New Testament canon, far from constituting the foundation of Christian unity, actually "provides the basis for the multiplicity of the confessions."[52] Yet, as Käsemann's critics have pointed out, such conflict is at least partially attributable to mistaken uses of the texts—for example, to insufficient attention to the context and scope of the individual traditions and claims, or to the tendency to fasten upon some one text or theme as the key by which all else is to be interpreted and judged. Problems can be traced to a failure to recognize the concrete limitations and the diverse functions of the scriptural material. But not all the evident conflicts will yield to treatment in these terms, even in principle. The Bible is an assemblage of greatly differing strategies for recollecting, interpreting, and sharing the community's witness concerning God. They defy harmonization. They do clash. It is impossible—not simply an overwhelmingly difficult task, but, at times, a logically impossible one—to affirm them all simultaneously. The fact that the church can use this collection of material as its canon does not preclude the possibility and necessity of sifting through its individual components with a critical eye, and making some judgments, in the light of the canon itself, as to the Christianness of some of its components, individually considered. To put the point briefly: Scripture as canon must rule the Christian use of scripture as source. The biblical canon assists the *critical* appropriation of biblical tradition. How this happens remains to be considered.

V
Christian Understanding
as a Critical Task

The distinction between the canonical use of the Bible and its use as a resource for contemporary Christian life and witness enables us to maintain a critical attitude toward the content of scripture without compromising its canonical status. "Canon" and "tradition" (or "canon" and "source") are not rival descriptions of scripture. They indicate its different uses. Thus, it would be a mistake to view a critical approach to the content of scripture as an unwarranted intrusion into the sacred precincts of the canon. The criticism of scriptural tradition does not threaten the scriptural canon. Indeed, scripture as canon actually mandates the critical examination of intrascriptural as well as extrascriptural tradition.

The testing of scripture by itself could, of course, be an empty exercise, like that of the man in Kierkegaard's story who bought a second copy of the newspaper to verify what he had read in his first copy. It is widely believed that scripture is able to be its own authentic critic only if one can posit a "canon within the canon," some criterion within scripture by which the Christianness of its individual components may be assessed. This is a notoriously ambiguous and elastic notion. The "canon within the canon" can be taken to mean a particular text or group of texts, or a particular theme or affirmation in scripture, or a phenomenon of some other sort which is held to be central, in some sense, to the biblical witness as a whole. The value of the notion is undeniable: It reminds interpreters that not every element within the Bible is "canonical" (i.e., authoritative for Christian witness) as it stands, simply by virtue of being between its covers. Determining the canonical force of the various elements of scripture is a part of the task of interpretation. Further, it maintains the Reformation principle that scripture is not to be interpreted or judged according to any extrinsic criterion or authority, but only by itself.

No doubt a way could be found to fit what has been said here about the canonical use of scripture into some version of the notion of a "canon within the canon." Still, insofar as the phrase itself seems to suggest that what is involved is the substitution of some portion of the biblical canon for the Bible itself—a suggestion that, however justifiable in a given instance, has done much to complicate discussion of the issue—it would seem best to avoid the phrase. Certainly it is correct to say that the canon (i.e., the criterion of Christian witness) is and remains in the canon (i.e., the collection of canonical scripture) and is not to be separated from it.[53] If "the canon within the canon" is only intended to refer thus to the *location* of the canon, to say that it is "in" these texts and not elsewhere, then it presents no difficulty. If it means, moreover, that the canon must be *sought* in these texts, that their canonical bearing must be discovered and cannot simply be assumed without further ado, then there is likewise no problem with it. But when the phrase is used to separate some more fully or truly canonical portions of scripture from less canonical portions, it may mislead—not because all of scripture is of equal canonical value and force, but because it suggests that the canon in scripture is a portion of scripture (or some formulation grounded in portions of scripture) which is above criticism. But if the canon "in" scripture is seen instead as scripture in a particular *use*, scripture construed and applied in such a way as to enable the discernment through it of the norm of Christian witness and understanding, then two important things follow: No portion of canonical scripture is excluded *a priori* from potential canonical usefulness; and no portion of scripture is above criticism in the light of the canon.

The classic twentieth-century engagement over this issue, inconclusive as it proved to be, occurred in the aftermath of the publication of the second edition of Karl Barth's *Epistle to the Romans*. Rudolf Bultmann, in his review of the book, charged that Barth's commentary was insufficiently critical of Paul. Even in Paul, Bultmann said, "there are other spirits speaking besides the *pneuma Christou*"; Barth's approach did not adequately provide for the necessary discrimination between the more and less authentically Christian elements in the letter. Barth replied in the preface to the third edition of his commentary: "I will certainly not argue with Bultmann which of us is the more radical, but I must still really go a little further than he does and say that what speaks in the Letter to the Romans is nothing but the 'others,' the various 'spirits' which he adduces, such as the Jewish, the popular Christian, the Hellenistic, and others. Or, at what place could one point his finger with the observation that *there* assuredly the *pneuma Christou* speaks?" Barth went on to state his point in terms of the familiar distinction between letter and spirit. One does not dismiss certain passages as "letter" and accept others as "spirit." Rather, one acknowledges that it is *all* "letter"—but also that the spirit may speak in any of it.[54]

Barth is here resisting the notion of a canon within the canon, and is taking the letter/spirit distinction as a way of saying that the key issue is not concerning *portions* of scripture, but *uses* of scripture. Without entering any further into the merits of either side in this exchange, the cruciality of this emphasis of Barth's on the function of the words of the text should be clear. The same text which is indisputably the work of a particular human author with particular views, insights, and limitations may also become the vehicle of God's word; the text that appears most transparent to a revealed word may become "letter." This does not mean that we are at the mercy of the text as it strikes us at any moment. It means that we cannot simply locate the canon in any particular form of words, henceforth exempt from criticism. To be sure, the canon is bound to the words of scripture. But scripture is activated as canon only in the coincidence of letter and spirit. The canon subsists in scripture, to be realized in the event of its explication.[55]

This is why it is vital to pay attention to what is involved in explicating the Bible as canon. We have seen that the canonical use of the Bible requires of the interpreter a basic decision as to how the Bible may be construed as a whole, that is, as a singular canon. That decision presupposes some consideration of the purpose for which and the circumstances in which the canon is to be used, as well as of the character of the biblical materials themselves; and it leads to a working understanding of the inner configurations, interrelationships, and relative functions of the various components of the canon. The Bible as canon is not simply the sum of its parts. It is the new instrument produced by the working together of these parts when they are taken in a certain way, that is, according to the canonical construal which has been adopted. Just as table salt is not merely the sum of certain proportions of sodium and chlorine, so the canon is not merely an anthology of documents, but, rather, the product of their interaction.

One major implication of this, of course, is that canonical authority does not belong to the individual components of the canon in themselves. Any biblical text has the possibility of canonical authority only indirectly, as it either contributes to or expresses the sense of the canon as a whole. There are texts which contribute to the constitution of the canon, that is, which enhance or illumine its witness somehow, but which could hardly be understood to be expressive of the sense of the canon in themselves. Their elimination from the canon might diminish its witness or its effectiveness in one way or another, even though they are in no way representative of the canon. There are some among these whose anomalous status may even be the clue to their canonical role: like the friends of Job, they provoke to deeper consideration even though—or just because—their own proposals are unsatisfactory. Aspects of both Old and New Testament tradition may find their canonical use in this way.[56] These disparate elements are not to be "harmonized" into some innocuous consensus. Their function is, rather, to stimulate more thorough reflection and more honest engagement, and thus, to enable a clearer and more lively apprehension of the canonical witness and its implications. Such a text may serve as a catalyst in the strict sense, permitting something to happen while remaining distinct from, even foreign to, the result.

Other texts may more properly bear the task of representing canonical witness on a certain point—for example, in preaching or in theological argument. Here still, it is vital to resist identifying the canon with a particular text, however apt it seems. But with this caution in mind, there can be no question that a given text may lend itself to the role of canonical representative, either in one instance or over a considerable range. Some texts seem perennially unsuited to such service, while still others may, for one reason or another, gain or lose this representativeness in particular situations. As Ernst Käsemann has pointed out, it is one thing to say that all of scripture should be heard, but it is something else to say that one can or should *preach* it all.[57]

All of scripture should be heard if its canonical sense is to be most fully discerned. But the canon itself raises serious questions as to the propriety of "preaching" some of its constituent parts, that is, of commending and explicating them as sources or standards of authentic Christian witness.

This distinction of Käsemann's points to the broader task of a critical theological exegesis of scripture. It would be shortsighted to regard scripture only as raw material for the canon, that is, to evaluate it solely in terms of its usefulness in constituting or representing canonical witness. The canonical function is only one function of scripture; and vital as it is, it should not preoccupy us to such an extent that we neglect scripture in its more ordinary "traditioning" function, or, for that matter, in other functions which it may be found to serve. Nor should we conflate those functions so that all that scripture yields is thought to have canonical force.

Release from the notion that everything to be found in scripture has canonical force as it stands means freedom to admit and to explore the immensely varied content of these texts. The texts and their constituent traditions are no longer regarded only as the components of "a book with which one feels bound always to agree," to recall William Newton Clarke's phrase. They can be heard without any prior obligation on the hearer's part to give assent. Assent, or its withholding, may be entirely beside the point, if one's purpose is to find out what a particular text has to say. Even when the understanding at which one aims requires considerable personal engagement with the text, this engagement can and must have a tentative, heuristic cast, so far as theological exegesis is concerned. That is, an interpreter is free to study the text, to interact with it in all sorts of imaginative ways, to discover in the text, or in that interaction, new data, new insights, new possibilities for self-understanding or for the life of the church, all in a spirit of inquiry and with some real hope that the results of this exploration will be useful. There is much to recover beneath the received text of scripture as well as within it, and there is much to discover through the application to the text of new minds and new ways of reading. The canonicity of the text does not hinder any of these ventures.

Nor, of course, does the fact that it is the Bible which is being studied make the results of its study, by whatever means, authentically Christian. It is well to distinguish, as Jonathan Edwards did, between what is occasioned by the Bible and what is properly derived from it.[58] Not everything which the text occasions or makes possible is thereby authorized as Christian. (While Käsemann's distinction focuses on the content of scripture, Edwards' stresses its uses. We may take them as complementing each other in this regard.) The canon as such comes in at the point of the interpreter's judgment as to the "Christian aptness" of the possibilities these varied inquiries open up: that is, as to how (if at all) the results of a given study or technique may be used in ways consistent with the canonical self-disclosure of God. That a structural study of a gospel yields certain data, or that a parable may be read in such a way as to evoke a certain judgment, is a matter upon which the canon has no authority to pronounce. But whether the use one proposes to make of that data or of that reading is a properly Christian use is a question to which the canon may speak, in its own way.

The principal aim of a Christian understanding of scripture is the knowledge of God. The canon serves chiefly as the criterion of that knowledge: whatever we know, or think we know, of God is to be assayed in the fire of that self-disclosure of God to which scripture as canon attests. But scripture conveys other kinds of knowledge and invites other uses as well, and a Christian understanding of scripture is also concerned to receive this knowledge and to gain acquaintance with these uses so as to deal with them appropriately. Again, all of scripture is to be "heard," and in a variety of ways. And although not all that is heard may be rightly "preached," or put to the service of Christian witness and understanding, there is much in scripture beyond its canonical witness which has, or should have, a justifiably important place in the life and thought of the church. There are also elements of the biblical tradition which deserve clear criticism in the light of the canon, and whose unwarranted influence upon the church needs to be called into question.

For example: There appears to be more than one pattern of church order and leadership displayed and commended in the New Testament. None of the patterns may be strictly normative, in the sense of bearing canonical authorization. Any of them may be useful in stimulating reflection upon the possibilities and problems of ecclesiastical polity. If there were only one such pattern commonly acknowledged throughout the New Testament, it would still not be normative in that sense. That is, unless it could be shown somehow to be the only pattern of church order consistent with the canonical witness concerning God, it would have to be acknowledged only as one possibility. However strong the credentials of that pattern as a hallowed precedent with demonstrated effectiveness and a wealth of additional benefits, it is still possible that another situation may call for a reconsideration of the whole issue of church order and authority, just as it is more than possible that the received pattern was attended by its own liabilities and problems along with its manifest advantages. A consideration of past, present, and future church order certainly must not disregard the biblical precedents; but it must take care not to mistake every strand of biblical tradition for canonical witness. The fundamental question to be faced is not, What pattern of church order is found in the Bible? but rather,

What pattern of church order is, under these circumstances, most consistent with the identity of the One to whom the church is called to bear witness? Circumstances alone do not dictate a proper resolution of this question, nor does biblical precedent alone, but both should be considered in the search for an understanding of the church's common life which is "scriptural" in the proper sense, that is, in accord with the canon of scripture.

Or again: Different strands of biblical material seem to evince different attitudes toward the phenomena we commonly designate as "other religions." Even if we could harmonize these into a single "biblical view" of these phenomena, that view would not yet have canonical force. This is not to denigrate the potential value of any of these views, or of their product, to the task of attaining a Christian understanding of "other religions." It is only to claim that the biblical view or views of these phenomena must themselves be evaluated in the light of the canon before they can be responsibly appropriated. Such evaluation must take into account the circumstances under which the views were formed, the extent and quality of the information upon which they were based, the concerns they express, and the scope of their intentions. But a contemporary theological engagement with the actuality of "other religions" must go beyond the question of what the Bible says about them—however carefully that question is analyzed and answered—to the more fundamental question of what attitudes toward these phenomena (or, better: toward a particular instance in certain circumstances), are consistent with the canonical witness concerning the reality of God. Here too, as in the case of patterns of church order, there are data to be considered which the canon itself can neither provide nor confirm, for example, as to what life as a Buddhist or as a Muslim actually involves. The canon may permit a judgment as to how those involvements may bear upon the relationships of such persons and communities to God, but a particular judgment must be conditioned upon the validity of data beyond the canon's own scope.

These examples only hint at the sort of thoroughly critical appropriation of biblical traditions which a clear awareness of the nature and scope of the canonical function of the Bible makes possible. These traditions form the common memory and linguistic heritage of the Christian community, which is nourished in every way by them. They are the common stock giving continuity to its life and expression. But with regard to any given element of biblical tradition, we are not only permitted but obliged to give it careful scrutiny, measuring it by the canon, before we permit it any constitutive role in the contemporary understanding of Christian witness. That each such element is part of the Christian heritage cannot be denied; that each is "truly Christian" in the normative sense must not be so easily granted. The questionableness of some aspects of biblical tradition may be readily apparent to us, such as the cosmological assumptions of Genesis. Others may be so much a part of the fabric of our own consciousness and social structure that they can be brought into view only through a painstaking analysis which is also a painful self-analysis, for example, the relationship between the sexes—and particularly the subordination of women—which is ingrained in the biblical traditions as it is in the cultures influenced by those traditions (though certainly not only in them).

Our complicity in the maintenance of such elements of tradition may block our discernment of the canonical witness with its opposition to them. And that is why the task of critical theological exegesis entails rigorous self-criticism and the criticism of the social, political, and cultural arrangements, perspectives, and values of the interpreter, no less than the critical examination of the text in its whole context. Only in this way can the third moment of exegesis, that of "application," be at all adequately realized. A recovery of the canonical function of scripture in its distinctiveness from and relationship to the use of biblical tradition does not promise any simplification of the exegetical task— as if, with canon in hand, the interpreter need not trouble any further over the exegetical issues that have exercised interpreters since the emergence of modern historical awareness. But it does promise a theological criterion for the evaluation and use of the results of such exegesis, of whatever form.

Obviously, not every reader of the Bible has the knowledge and skills necessary to explore its many dimensions and to make them accessible for critical reflection and appropriation. Not everyone is in a position to hear the testimony of the sources within the texts, or even to hear the texts themselves as their first audiences heard them. Not everyone is master of the philosophical and technical resources which have permitted some interpreters to develop intriguing and unconventional ways of listening to and interacting with the texts. For the fruits of such inquiries, some of which may be of considerable importance to our ongoing reflection upon Christian life and witness, we are fundamentally dependent upon specialists.

This is no cause for lamentation. The idea that every believer should have direct access to the message of scripture along with the right of private judgment as to its content has come more and more to be seen, and rightly so, as a matter of principle rather than of fact. Properly qualified, it amounts to the claim that every believer with the requisite exegetical preparation may be a competent interpreter. Although this necessary proviso is sometimes decried as the surrender of a Reformation principle and a return to interpretation by authority (the "new papacy" of scholars), this is surely a mistaken charge. There is a vast difference between a competence defined by demonstrable exegetical abilities and a competence bestowed by ecclesiastical status. That the responsible handling of scripture requires the former has been generally acknowledged in the Protestant tradition, however firmly the latter has been excluded. The specialization and professionalization of exegetical scholarship has been a direct consequence of that acknowledgment, and is a development to be affirmed without resentment, insofar as it has established the conditions under which potentially useful new understandings of the texts may be achieved.

And yet the Christian understanding of scripture cannot be wholly delegated to specialists. To state this point positively: There is a discipline of interpretation which belongs to the Christian community at large, and severally to its members. It is important to put this point positively, because of the prevalence of the erroneous impression that the only alternative to specialized biblical scholarship is an undisciplined and uncritical reading of the texts.

We have noted the impact of modern historical consciousness upon the notion of the "literal sense" of scripture, and the consequent erosion of confidence in the ordinary reader's competence to understand the Bible at all. Granted the equation of "literal sense" with "original meaning," and given the great temporal and cultural distance separating the biblical texts from a present-day reader, it seems inevitable that interpretation should become the business of those few who are equipped by scholarly preparation and experience to search out that meaning and to retail it to the rest of us.

But this identification of literal sense with original meaning is only one option among several. A decision as to what is to count as the literal sense of a text is grounded in what one takes to be the relevant *usus loquendi.* That is, "the literal sense" is as context dependent a term as "the meaning of the text." It is always appropriate to ask for some further specification as to how the term is operating in a given case. In the course of medieval discussion of exegesis, for instance, the "literal sense" was defined in several different, though not necessarily mutually exclusive ways, for example, as what the human author of a text meant by it, or as what God means by it, or as what the church means by it.[59] Each option involves its own assumptions as to how authorship, or the production of sense, is to be conceived. Whose use of these words is to be heeded or given priority as setting the context within which their plain meaning is to be determined? A commitment to the literal sense per se does not establish the course of interpretation until this question is settled, since the answer to it determines the *usus loquendi* in which the literal sense is to be sought.

However else the meaning of the term "the literal sense" may be specified, it has not ordinarily involved the supposition that whatever immediately strikes any reader as the meaning of a text—whatever seems "plain" to whatever reader happens along—is to be deemed its literal sense. If anything, the term has been invoked largely to guard against that sort of arbitrary subjectivism. The literal sense is plainly evident only to a reader who has a sufficient mastery of the *usus loquendi* in which the text has its life to read it without undue perplexity, and at the same time without imposing alien criteria upon its sense. The literal sense may be difficult or ambiguous, of course; and when it is, the competent reader will recognize that it is so.

If the *usus* to be heeded is that of the writer or first readers of a biblical text, then naturally we who do not share it are obliged to yield to those who, by virtue of their scholarly expertise, can manage to enter into it. Such an understanding of the Pauline kerygma, the prophetic message of Amos, or the historiography of the Chronicler, requires the sort of critical-historical reconstruction which only the specialist can provide. Yet, however valuable such an understanding may be to the church, there is a *usus* of scripture which has a prior claim to the church's attention, namely, the *usus* which establishes its canonical sense as God's self-disclosive Word. It is this canonical sense of the text which the church has the most reason to acknowledge as the literal sense of scripture, and that for two reasons. First, it is the theologically prior sense. Even though the canonical sense of a text may not be its historically original sense, it is its most basic sense in that the church is obliged to judge all other messages it may hear through these words in the light of this canonical Word. No other sense may supersede this one in the formation of Christian understanding. This is, after all, what is involved in acknowledging this sense as "canonical," and in acknowledging God to be the "primary author" of the canon. Whatever else the church may make of these texts, it first attends to what God is saying through them, and takes this as their primary sense.

Secondly, the canonical sense is that sense which the church is called to learn, to cultivate, to appropriate as the center and spring of its own life, to such a degree that the canonical sense *becomes* for it the plain meaning of the text. That is, it is the church's task so to master the canonical sense that it becomes, in practice as well as in principle, the measure of the church's own language; only then will the canonical sense function for Christian readers as the "literal sense" of the text, that is, the natural, obvious meaning as perceived by those who have made its *usus* their own.

How is this use to be acquired? Chiefly through a twofold discipline of canonical explication, on the one hand, and conceptual growth, on the other: through the practice of reading the scriptures in their canonical character, while simultaneously appropriating their concepts to form the fabric of one's own existence. Neither of these is a matter of a few hours' labor; they are coterminous with Christian existence itself, as the canon is heard and explicated in worship and preaching, study and meditation, and as its conceptuality as well as its perspective is taken on in the ordinary course of life. In another sense, of course, no amount of exertion will secure this end. It comes by grace or not at all. It would be misleading to think of this discipline as a means to an end, when it is more properly regarded as the medium in which Christian life is lived.

In any event, it is this discipline of understanding which belongs to Christians simply as Christians. The discernment of the canonical sense of scripture and the knowledge of God which it nourishes are the gift and responsibility of the Christian community and not only of a cadre of scholars. Although the capacity for such discernment and knowledge may vary widely, it is not the sort of capacity which scholarly excellence as such will necessarily foster. But it is a capacity that is nurtured in community. We are all dependent upon one another to stimulate and correct both our perceptions of the canonical witness and our attempts to live out of it. Technical biblical scholarship has its own contributions to make to this common task; but so does the experience of Christian people hearing and responding to the canonical witness under a great variety of circumstances.

Notes

1. William Newton Clarke, *The Use of the Scriptures in Theology* (Charles Scribner's Sons, 1905), p. 30.
2. Søren Kierkegaard, *Philosophical Fragments*, 2d ed., tr. David F. Swenson and Howard V. Hong (Princeton University Press, 1962), p. 51.
3. John Calvin, *Institutes of the Christian Religion*, ed. John T. McNeill, tr. and indexed Ford Lewis Battles (The Library of Christian Classics, Vol. XX) (Westminster Press, 1960), I. i. 1 (p. 35). Subsequent quotations from Calvin in this paragraph are from pp. 36 and 37 of this volume. The editorial note to this passage suggests that "existential apprehension" is the nearest contemporary equivalent to Calvin's "knowledge" in this connection. I am indebted to the masterly study by Edward A. Dowey, Jr., *The Knowledge of God in Calvin's Theology* (Columbia University Press, 1951).
4. Karl Barth, *Church Dogmatics*, Vol. II, Part 1, ed. G. W. Bromiley and T. F. Torrance (Edinburgh: T. & T. Clark, 1957), p. 61.
5. Ludwig Wittgenstein, *Remarks on the Foundation of Mathematics*, ed. G. H. von Wright, Rush Rhees, and G. E. M. Anscombe, tr. G. E. M. Anscombe (Oxford: Basil Blackwell, Publisher, 1964), p. 195e.
6. Gilbert Ryle, "On Forgetting the Difference Between Right and Wrong," *Collected Papers, Vol. II: Collected Essays, 1929–1968* (Barnes & Noble, 1971), pp. 381–390. On concepts, see also "Knowing How and Knowing That" and "Thinking Thoughts and Having Concepts," in the same volume.

7. Calvin, *Institutes*, I. ii. 2 (p. 41); see Dowey, *The Knowledge of God in Calvin's Theology*, pp. 4–5.

8. Brevard S. Childs, "The Sensus Literalis of Scripture: An Ancient and Modern Problem," in *Beiträge zur alttestamentlichen Theologie: Festschrift für Walther Zimmerli zum 70. Geburtstag*, ed. Herbert Donner et al. (Göttingen: Vandenhoeck & Ruprecht, 1977), pp. 80–93.

9. James Boswell, *The Life of Samuel Johnson*, entry for September 19, 1777.

10. Gerhard Ebeling, "Word of God and Hermeneutics," *Word and Faith*, tr. James W. Leitch (Fortress Press, 1963), p. 318.

11. Ludwig Wittgenstein, *Philosophical Investigations*, 3d ed., ed. G. E. M. Anscombe and Rush Rhees, tr. G. E. M. Anscombe (Macmillan Co., 1958), p. 79e.

12. On W. Robertson Smith, see Childs, "The Sensus Literalis of Scripture," pp. 89–90. Frederic W. Farrar, *History of Interpretation* (Baker Book House, 1961), Lecture VIII.

13. Hans W. Frei, *The Eclipse of Biblical Narrative* (Yale University Press, 1974).

14. See, e.g., Wolfhart Pannenberg, "The Crisis of the Scripture Principle," *Basic Questions in Theology*, Vol. I, tr. George H. Kehm (Fortress Press, 1970), pp. 1–14.

15. H. Richard Niebuhr, *The Meaning of Revelation* (Macmillan Co., 1962), p. 137.

16. A recent heir of this tradition says of his own investigation: "It asks (to put it in Kantian terms): How is understanding possible? This is a question which precedes any action of understanding on the part of subjectivity." (Hans-Georg Gadamer, *Truth and Method*, ed. Garrett Barden and John Cumming, p. xviii; Seabury Press, 1975.)

17. For a more sustained discussion of the philosophical issues surrounding "understanding," and of this turn in its conceptualization, see Charles M. Wood, *Theory and Religious Understanding* (Scholars Press, 1975).

18. W. B. Gallie, *Philosophy and the Historical Understanding*, 2d ed. (Schocken Books, 1968), p. 48.

19. This mistranslation stems from the Septuagint.

20. Cf. Karl Barth's arrangement of his discussion of theological exegesis under these three heads in *Church Dogmatics*, Vol. I, Part 2, ed. G. W. Bromiley and T. F. Torrance (Edinburgh: T. & T. Clark, 1956), pp. 721ff.

21. Johann August Ernesti, *Elementary Principles of Interpretation*, tr. Moses Stuart, 3d ed. (Andover and New York: Gould and Newman, 1838), sec. 27, p. 13.

22. Ibid., sec. 33, p. 16.

23. Ibid., secs. 4–10, pp. 2–5.

24. F. D. E. Schleiermacher, *Hermeneutics: The Handwritten Manuscripts*, ed. Heinz Kimmerle, tr. James Duke and Jack Forstman (Scholars Press, 1977), p. 41. I have omitted the translators' bracketed translation of *subtilitas explicandi* as "exactness of explication," to reduce confusion in the citation.

25. Ernesti, *Elementary Principles of Interpretation*, sec. 16, p. 8.

26. For a brief discussion of Ernesti in his intellectual context, see Wilhelm Dilthey, *Leben Schleiermachers*, in *Gesammelte Schriften*, XIV, 2 (Göttingen: Vandenhoeck & Ruprecht, 1966), pp. 640ff.

27. E. D. Hirsch, Jr., *The Aims of Interpretation* (University of Chicago Press, 1976), p. 33. Hirsch is probably the most prominent contemporary advocate of a hermeneutical position similar to Ernesti's, first elaborated in his *Validity in Interpretation* (Yale University Press, 1967) and refined in some respects in the essays collected in Part One of *The Aims of Interpretation*.

28. Ernesti, *Elementary Principles of Interpretation*, sec. 38, p. 19, and sec. 142, pp. 67–68.

29. James Barr, "Trends and Prospects in Biblical Theology," *Journal of Theological Studies*, Vol. 25 (1974), p. 274.

30. Ernesti, *Elementary Principles of Interpretation*, sec. 38, p. 19.

31. Charles M. Wood, "Word of God and Truth," *Encounter*, Vol. 41 (1980), pp. 219–227.

32. Barth, *Church Dogmatics*, Vol. I, Part 2, p. 727.

33. Jonathan Edwards, *Dissertation Concerning the End for Which God Created the World*, in *The Works of President Edwards*, 8th ed. (New York: Leavitt, Trow & Co., 1849), Vol. II, p. 253.

34. John Wisdom, "A Feature of Wittgenstein's Technique," *Paradox and Discovery* (Oxford: Basil Blackwell, Publisher, 1965), p. 102.

35. A remarkable sustained treatment of conceptual understanding and rationality from this perspective is Stephen Toulmin, *Human Understanding*, Vol. I: *The Collective Use and Evolution of Concepts* (Princeton University Press, 1972). On the hermeneutical implications of the point, see further Albert William Levi, "De Interpretatione: Cognition and Context in the History of Ideas," *Critical Inquiry*, Vol. 3 (1976), pp. 153–178.

36. See Louis O. Mink, "Narrative Form as Cognitive Instrument," in *The Writing of History: Literary Form and Historical Understanding,* ed. Robert H. Canary and Henry Kozicki (University of Wisconsin Press, 1978), pp. 129–149.

37. Calvin, *Institutes,* I. vi. 2 (p. 72). I have tried to suggest what "obedience" does not entail, and what sort of knowledge it yields, in "The Knowledge Born of Obedience," *Anglican Theological Review,* Vol. 61 (1979), pp. 331–340.

38. Gilbert Ryle, *The Concept of Mind* (Barnes & Noble, 1949), p. 43.

39. Barth, *Church Dogmatics,* Vol. I, Part 2, p. 737.

40. David H. Kelsey, *The Uses of Scripture in Recent Theology* (Fortress Press, 1975), pp. 153–154. Kelsey helpfully distinguishes the question of the "Christianness" of a proposal from the question of its truth, and shows how appeals to scripture have their primary place in discussions of the first question.

41. Various perspectives on this cluster of issues are represented in the collection entitled *Das Neue Testament als Kanon,* ed. Ernst Käsemann (Göttingen: Vandenhoeck & Ruprecht, 1970). More recent literature involving both Old and New Testament canon questions amounts to a substantial bibliography.

42. For an overview of these developments, see Hermann Strathmann, "Die Krisis des Kanons der Kirche: Joh. Gerhards und Joh. Sal. Semlers Erbe," in *Das Neue Testament als Kanon,* pp. 41–61.

43. The distinction drawn here differs from that proposed by A. C. Sundberg, Jr., "Towards a Revised History of the New Testament Canon," *Studia Evangelica,* Vol. IV, ed. F. L. Cross (Texte und Untersuchungen zur Geschichte der altchristlichen Literatur, 102; Berlin: Akademie-Verlag, 1968), pp. 453–454, for whom "scripture" designates religiously authoritative literature, while "canon" is a definitively closed collection of scripture.

44. Barr, "Trends and Prospects in Biblical Theology," p. 274.

45. Herbert Braun, "Hebt die heutige neutestamentlich-exegetische Forschung den Kanon auf?" in *Das Neue Testament als Kanon,* pp. 219–232, offers a telling critique of the notion of a "self-imposing" canon. The idealizing of the early church as a homogeneous community of exemplary faith and discernment persists, despite recent studies of the early Christian movement in its sociological, political, and cultural, as well as theological, di-

mensions. But it has persisted thus far despite the evidence of the New Testament itself, in any case.

46. Werner Georg Kümmel, "Notwendigkeit und Grenze des neutestamentlichen Kanons," *Das Neue Testament als Kanon*, p. 97.

47. The extent to which "inspiration" was felt to pertain to the life and witness of the church and not simply to its scripture is suggested by Everett Kalin, "The Inspired Community: A Glance at Canon History," *Concordia Theological Monthly*, Vol. 42 (1971), pp. 541–549.

48. Cf. David Kelsey's treatment of the construal of scripture as "rendering an agent" in *The Uses of Scripture in Recent Theology*, pp. 39–50. The relationships between this canonical story and "history" is, of course, a major question which the theological appropriation of this construal must confront. An insightful treatment of the question is Rudolf Smend, "Tradition and History: A Complex Relation," in *Tradition and Theology in the Old Testament*, ed. Douglas A. Knight (Fortress Press, 1977), pp. 49–68.

49. Robert Clyde Johnson, *Authority in Protestant Theology* (Westminster Press, 1959), pp. 14–15.

50. I am indebted to Schubert M. Ogden's discriminating treatment of the concept of authority in "The Authority of Scripture for Theology," *Interpretation*, Vol. 30 (July 1976), pp. 242–261, esp. pp. 245–248.

51. James A. Sanders, "Adaptable for Life: The Nature and Function of Canon," in *Magnalia Dei: The Mighty Acts of God*, ed. Frank M. Cross et al. (Doubleday & Co., 1976), p. 531.

52. Ernst Käsemann, "The Canon of the New Testament and the Unity of the Church," *Essays on New Testament Themes*, tr. W. J. Montague (London: SCM Press, 1964), p. 103. The original of this essay is reprinted, along with some of the critical discussions, in *Das Neue Testament als Kanon*.

53. See Inge Lönning, *"Kanon im Kanon": Zum dogmatischen Grundlagenproblem des neutestamentlichen Kanons* (Oslo: Universitetsforlaget and Munich: Chr. Kaiser Verlag, 1972), p. 110. For an illuminating critical synopsis of more recent discussion of this issue, see Wolfgang Schrage, "Die Frage nach der Mitte und dem Kanon im Kanon des Neuen Testaments in der neueren Diskussion," in *Rechtfertigung: Festschrift für Ernst Käsemann zum 70. Geburtstag*, ed. Johannes Friedrich, Wolfgang Pöhlmann, and Peter

Stuhlmacher (Tübingen: J. C. B. Mohr [Paul Siebeck] and Göttingen: Vandenhoeck & Ruprecht, 1976), pp. 415–442.

54. Barth's prefaces and Bultmann's review are assembled in translation in James M. Robinson, ed., *The Beginnings of Dialectic Theology*, Vol. I (John Knox Press, 1968), pp. 88–130. The lines quoted here from Bultmann appear on p. 120, those from Barth on p. 127.

55. On the letter/spirit relationship, see Charles M. Wood, "Finding the Life of a Text: Notes on the Explication of Scripture," *Scottish Journal of Theology*, Vol. 31 (1978) pp. 101–111.

56. For a provocative exploration of the function of such material, see Paul D. Hanson, "The Theological Significance of Contradiction Within the Book of the Covenant," in *Canon and Authority*, ed. George W. Coats and Burke O. Long (Fortress Press, 1977), pp. 110–131.

57. Ernst Käsemann, "Kritische Analyse," in *Das Neue Testament als Kanon*, p. 366.

58. "What deceives many of the less understanding and considerate sort of people, in this matter, seems to be this; that the Scripture is the Word of God, and has nothing in it which is wrong, but is pure and perfect; and therefore, those experiences which come from the Scripture must be right. But then it should be considered, affections may arise on *occasion* of the Scripture, and not *properly come from* the Scripture, as the genuine fruit of the Scripture, and by a right use of it; but from an abuse of it." (Jonathan Edwards, *Religious Affections*, ed. John E. Smith, p. 143; Yale University Press, 1959.)

59. See Part One of James Samuel Preus, *From Shadow to Promise: Old Testament Interpretation from Augustine to the Young Luther* (Harvard University Press, 1969), on the development of these positions.

Index